Preaching to Change Lives

WAYNE DEHONEY

Preaching to Change Lives

Broadman Press / Nashville, Tennessee

4222-23
ISBN: 0-8054-2223-4

Dewey Decimal Classification: 252
Library of Congress Catalog Card number: 74-80339
Printed in the United States of America

To the beloved members
of the Walnut Street Baptist Church
of Louisville, Kentucky, where,
by the power of the Holy Spirit,
miracles of grace happen every week

Contents

INTRODUCTION

To my way of thinking, the purpose of evangelical preaching is to *change lives!* To do so . . .

That preaching must be *authoritative.* It is a clarion trumpet "thus saith the Lord." It must be biblically based, sound in doctrine, and have the ring of authenticity and personal experience.

That preaching must be *relevant.* But that relevancy is *person-focused* rather than *issue-oriented.* For on every pew sits a broken heart, a guilty conscience, a lonely spirit, a lost soul. And these have come to hear the Word of God from the man of God.

That preaching must be *good news.* Man is a sinner and lost; that's bad news! The world is going to the devil; that's bad news! But "a most wonderful thing has happened. God was in Christ reconciling the world unto himself. If we confess our sins, he is faithful and just to forgive us our sins. Unto as many as believed gave he power to become the sons of God." That's GOOD NEWS! *That* is our message. It is a message of positives, not negatives; of assurances, not doubts; of "this *one* thing I *know,*" not "these *many things* I *don't know.*"

That preaching must be *evangelistic.* It demands of the hearer an immediate *confrontation.* For Christianity is not essentially institutional although it does have community and structure. Christianity is not essentially theological, although it does have a theology. Christianity is not essentially creedal, although it does have certain affirmations of faith. Christianity is not essentially ritual, although it does have patterns and forms of worship. Christianity is essentially *experiential*—a personal experience with the living Christ. Evangelical preaching, regardless of its text and theme, ends with the hearer facing the ultimate question of Pilate, "What will *you* do then with Jesus?"

These sermons are not essays prepared for publication. These are sermons *preached* in the pulpit of the Walnut Street Baptist Church of Louisville, Kentucky. These sermons represent a faltering human effort to measure up to these ideals in evangelical preaching. Bathed by the power of the Holy Spirit, these are sermons *that have changed lives!*

WAYNE DEHONEY

I

The Gospel in Miniature

Revelation 1:5-6

I once saw in a novelty shop a "postage stamp" Bible. It was the complete Scriptures reduced to a tiny book a half-inch thick and the dimensions of a postage stamp—but clearly readable with a magnifying glass!

What if you were asked to produce a postage stamp gospel—that is, to reduce the declaration of your faith in Christ to a single statement that embodied all the essential elements of the gospel?

Some might simply recite the Apostle's Creed, "I believe in God the Father Almighty . . . etc." Others would reject a creedal statement and say, "The whole of the gospel is to be found in the Sermon on the Mount." Yet another might reduce the gospel to a single sentence,"I think the Golden Rule is enough: do unto others as you would that others do unto you."

This is one of the contemporary theological controversies of our day. Exactly what *is* the gospel anyway? Is it "hot sermons on sin"? Or " a cup of cold water" given in Jesus' name? Is it social activism? Preaching? The programs of the institutional church? Organized political efforts to change the structure of society?

The word "gospel" means simply good news. What, then, is the good news that we have to share? It is something that we have *experienced* that has made our hearts to rejoice. It is a change of heart and nature that has made living different. It is a quality of life that has put us on the mountaintop regardless of our job, our health, our station in life, our fortune or misfortune. It is something that has happened to give us victory over sin and the grave. At the center of this experience is the living reality of a person, Jesus Christ. Who is this Jesus? What has he done for us? What should we do for him? Find the answer to these questions and you have the gospel in a nutshell.

In a few dozen words in Revelation 1:5-7 John gives a succinct answer to these essential questions and gives us our postage stamp gospel. It is a simple statement of faith that overarches the eternal purpose and will of God from the beginning of time to this very moment as you are face to face with Jesus Christ.

Who He Is

If a stranger asks, "Give me the keys to your car," you would rightly demand, "Who are you? What do you want with my car?" If I demanded, "Sign a blank check on your bank account and give it to me," you would rightly question my authority to claim possession of all your money. Yet here is one who asks for a commitment of more than your car or your possessions. He demands of you your whole being, a total commitment of life itself, your very soul!

Who then is this Jesus who makes such claims on our lives? John says that he is Jesus Christ "who is the *faithful witness.*" A witness is one called into court to give firsthand testimony. Hearsay or secondhand evidence is not valid. Personal ideas and judgments are not acceptable! So John declares that Jesus Christ is a faithful witness, qualified to testify about God, heaven, hell, death, the grave, eternal life because of firsthand personal experience.

Other religions may exhibit their religious heritage, their sacred writings, their ethical structures. Other prophets may testify of their religious and philosophical concepts about God, and spiritual and eternal matters. All such religions are the same in the sense that they are efforts of finite man *reaching up* after infinite God. But only in Christianity do we have the bold affirmation that

God has *reached down* to man to reveal himself in the flesh and dwelt among us in Jesus Christ.

Every other religion is simply an extension of man's intellect, man's reason, man's philosophy, man's moral nature, man's divine instinct, reaching up to find God and formulating and fabricating a manmade system of religion, ethics, and worship. But John says only Jesus Christ is the faithful witness to these things. For he was *with* God, came *from* God, and was Emmanuel, *God with us.* He testifies of God because of firsthand experience. Jesus Christ is the faithful true witness of all things concerning God, life, man, and eternity.

Jesus is also "the first begotten of the dead." The *fact* of his resurrection validates this claim that he is God in the flesh. The empty tomb is an irrefutable historical fact. The resurrected Christ was seen on ten different occasions by many reputable witnesses.

This Jesus was the *first* begotten of the dead . . . others shall follow in this victory over death and the grave. Because he lives, we shall live also! Death shall not have final dominion over those who follow him. The resurrection power that brought Jesus Christ forth the first begotten of the dead will also bring us forth alive.

Jesus Christ is "the *prince of the kings of this earth.*" Where is he now? What is he doing since the resurrection? John says he is reigning at the right hand of the throne of God. All the affairs of this world are under his control. Mightier than any army that ever marched, more powerful than any Caesar who ever reigned, greater than any parliament that ever sat, he is the *prince* of the kings and powers of this earth.

This is the Jesus Christ that claimed you, that stands in judgment before your will, asking for a commitment and surrender of your life to him.

What He Has Done

After declaring who Jesus is, John then tells *what he has done,* and what he will do for you and me. John uses three strong verbs to describe what Jesus has done: *loved, washed,* and *made!*

Loved Us

John says, "Unto him that hath *loved* us." John testifies that this was the beginning point of his new relationship with God—not that "I love God" but that through Jesus Christ I realized how much "God loved me."

All men instinctively seek to know God and to love him. We are made by God, in the image in God, for fellowship with God. But sin has defaced that image and separated us from God. And the nameless longing of every human heart is to find God and be restored to fellowhip with him. Every culture and every civilization that the world has ever known has had some kind of religion that taught men to seek God, to love God, and to solicit his favor and friendship by sacrifice and service to him. Fear of the wrath of God, the power of God, the judgment of God upon their sins often motivated this service and love. But the revolutionary revelation of Jesus Christ is that God is not angry with us—it is not his desire to see us suffer for our sins—his consuming passion is to love us!

1. Furthermore the Bible says that with God it was *first* love. Lovers sometimes argue as to which one loved first. A boy says, "I was standing on the steps that first day at school when you walked by. It was love at first sight—I fell in love with you before you ever knew my name!" But the girl coyly replies, "That's what you think! I had already fallen for you in that first class period. I had to walk by those steps three times before I caught your eye!" But with us and God there is no argument! God loved us first before we ever knew his name. While we were yet sinners, Christ died for our sins, the Bible says.

2. It is not only first love, but *continuing* love. A more proper translation of this Greek verb is "loveth us," rather than "loved." The good news of the gospel is not merely the declaration of one momentous demonstration of love by God 2,000 years ago

when the Word became flesh and dwelt among us at Bethlehem—and when the Lamb of God died for our sins on the cross at Calvary. It is not a *past tense* love, demonstrated at this one glorious point in time and in space. The Greek verb is *present tense linear action.* He loved us *then,* at Calvary. But he has continued to love us to this very day. And he will *keep on* loving us without end!

And because he so loves fully as much today as he did when he died on the cross, I know he cares for us today! As I walked through the wards of a veteran's hospital the nurse said, "These are society's forgotten men! Some are here from World War I and have not received a visitor or a letter in many years. They have been forsaken by kinsmen and forgotten by the world." Sometimes you may feel that you have been forsaken and forgotten by all who care. But remember, you are not forsaken or forgotten by Christ. Whoever you are, know that this day he loves you! God cares for you! John says he is the one that "loveth us" always!

3. It is first love, continuing love, and *universal* love. In Paris, Texas, I was told a moving story about Daddy Buckner, founder of the famous Buckner's Orphans Home. The institution is the lengthened shadow of this beloved Baptist preacher. One day a girl named Mary was brought to the home. Her family had died in a fire. Mary herself was severly burned, her face scarred, one arm and leg crippled.

It was Daddy Buckner's practice to tell Bible stories to the children as they gathered under an oak tree after the evening meal. The children pressed around him vying for the privilege of sitting in his lap and touching him as he sat in their midst. But Mary always stayed on the outside of the circle away from the other children and far from him.

One evening as he sent the other children to bed, he said to Mary, "Come here, I want to talk to you." Timidly and reluctantly she moved sideways toward him, keeping the scarred side of her face and body turned from him. Daddy Buckner reached out, pulled her onto his lap and asked, "What is the matter, Mary? Aren't you happy here?" She answered, "Yes, Daddy Buckner, I am very happy—for this is the only home I have." "Then, don't you love me?" he asked. She replied, "Yes, I love you more than anyone else in the world—you're the only daddy I have!" "Then," he asked, "why don't you want to sit on my lap, and get close to me like the other children do?"

She paused for a long time, and then said, "I didn't think you wanted a scarred, ugly, crippled little girl like me sitting on your lap close to you." The great Christian man turned her scarred face toward him, and kissed it and drew her twisted arm and leg close into his arms and said, "Mary, always remember this—I love you. And when I look at you, I don't see the scars on your face. I just see a little girl without a daddy who needs me to love you. And you look like *all* the other little boys and girls to me—*for I love you all alike.*"

See Jesus hanging on the cross! Gathered there are his friends, a handful of faithful disciples, his mother. Surely Jesus said in his heart, "I love them—and, Father, bless them." But at his feet also were the cruel wicked men who crucified him, mocked him, lied about him, rejected him. He stretched his arms a little further on the cross and prayed, "Father, I love them, *too*—for they are *all alike* in my sight, frail, sinful men needing a Savior—Father, forgive them—forgive them *all* for they know not what they do."

At that moment on the cross Jesus reached and planted a kiss on the face of, not just the good, lovable, decent people—but on the face of the ugliest sin-scarred life, the most wicked sinner, the most dissolute reprobate, the most hardened heart the world has ever known. He says, "I love you even as I love the finest, most decent person that ever lived. You are *all alike* in my sight—sinners needing the love of a Savior to die for them."

You may so sin as to go beyond the love of your parents, beyond the love of your friends, beyond the love of all others in this world! But you can never so sin that you slip beyond the love of Christ! John says that Jesus is the one that "loveth us!" That is the beginning of the good news!

Washed Us

Then John says that through this love in action, he has "*washed us* from our sins in his own blood." As water cleanses our bodies, so his blood has *cleansed* our soul of the filth of sin!

Yet another translation of the Greek verb is "loose." Surely, he has "washed us" but he has also "loosed us from our sins by the power of his blood." An Old Testament verse promises, "Though your sins be as scarlet, they shall become white as snow." I had always thought of scarlet as merely symbolic of the dark solid coloring of massive sin that is washed away by Christ's blood.

But then I read somewhere that scarlet was permanent dye that indelibly marked every fiber of the fabric. As long as one thread of the fabric remained, the stain of the dye would be there! So sin has permeated the very warp and woof of our nature. Not a shred has escaped sin's permanent contamination. Every fiber of our humanity is impregnated by sin. Sin is ingrained in our appetite, desire, will, emotion, mind! The oldtime preachers spoke of the "total depravity of man." They did not mean that all men were as bad as they could possibly be—but that every faculty of the human personality has been totally contaminated by sin.

It is the picture of not merely a slave shackled hand and foot by chains. Every cell in the body of the slave, every facet of the slave's personality is in bondage and shackled by sin. Marked *as by scarlet,* no earthly power can cleanse or loose man from his sins. But John triumphantly shouts, "The blood of Jesus Christ has loosed us." And it is as the Bible promises, "the blood of Christ cleanses us from all sin" (1 John 1:7).

Made Us Kings and Priests

Then John says that this love expressed through the blood of

Christ has cleansed us to make of us new creatures. He has "made us kings and priests unto God his father."

The Italian dictator, Mussolini, harangued his black-shirted youth of the fascist movement during World War II to "Remember—you are sons of the wolf!" In recalling the legend of the founding of Rome by the brothers, Romulus and Remus who were nursed by a mother wolf, he was challenging the young men to be tough, strong, efficient, physical animals. I recall seeing newsreels of those "sons of the wolf" demonstrating their physical prowess and courage by diving over barricades of unsheathed bayonets, clearing the razor-like blades by only inches.

Now some would say that you are really only—a son of the wolf. You are merely an eating, drinking, love-making animal at the top of a mechanical evolutionary ladder. They would say you are only *quantitatively* different than the wolf—not *qualitatively* different! They would say that your *destiny* is the same dark clay pit as the dead body of a dog!

But the good news of the gospel of Jesus Christ is that you have a higher destiny. Through Jesus Christ you are made a king and a priest unto God, his father, a royal member of the heavenly family. So the great apostle Paul says, "If any man be in Christ, he is a new creature: old things are passed away; behold, all things are become new" (2 Cor. 5:17).

What Must We Do for Him?

This is *who Jesus is!* This is *what he has done* for us! Then John says *this is what we must do for him,* "Unto him be glory and dominion forever and ever."

First, we are to take this new life in Christ and so live it to glorify God in our daily lives. In word and deed, in purpose and plan, in joy and sorrow, in sickness and health, in work and pleasure, fellow Christian, do "all to the glory of God!"

A missionary nurse was cleaning the pus-infected sore on the stubby deformed arm of a leper in a bush clinic in Africa. The sight was nauseating! The stench overwhelming! With loving patience she pulled the filthy bandages back and applied the cleansing swabs. With her was a friend who was employed in the diplomatic corps of her country. He was stationed in the capital, had known her in the States, and was visiting with her. He turned away from the gruesome sight and said, "I wouldn't do that for a million dollars!" The girl quickly replied, "Neither would I!" Then in almost a lyric song she said, "But I gladly do it for the glory of God!" This is the motivation for all that we do for him as Christians. No monetary reward could ever buy the martyrs' blood! But service, to the glory of God, compels and constrains us—if this is truly *who Jesus is*, and this is *what he has done for us*. "Unto him be glory!"

Then, let every person give him "dominion." Dominion means lordship. You are saved when you receive Christ as your Savior from sin and make him *Lord* of your life!

Stuart Hamblin was a rough, hard-living cowboy, Hollywood actor, and radio disc jockey. One night he went to a Billy Graham revival meeting and was converted. Later he was witnessing to his fellow actor, John Wayne, of his newfound life in Jesus Christ. He said, "John, you should give your life to the Lord, too! It's no *secret* what God can do. What he has done for *others*, he can do for you!" The fellow actor said, "What a beautiful thought, Stu; you ought to write a song about that!" And so from the heart and lips of a converted Hollywood actor came the eloquent testimony in song, "It Is No Secret What God Can Do."

Thus a twentieth-century disciple and a first-century disciple join in singing a beautiful invitation hymn about Jesus Christ who "Hath loved us, washed us from our sins in his own blood and made us kings and priests unto God and his Father." They both urge you to give him "glory and dominion" in your life by receiving him as Lord and Savior.

II

What in the Devil Have We Been Doing?

Romans 5:6-11

A minister was speaking in a college chapel where one student asked another, "What is this business of sin he's talking about?" The other replied, "I think it has something to do with Adam and Eve." The first student concluded, "Oh, then it doesn't have anything to do with us!"

But I assure you that this business of sin does vitally pertain to you and me.

The Reality of Sin

Sin is no ghost conjured up by a preacher to frighten you.

Sin is a *reality* that you face every day. On that key ring in your pocket is a house key. Why did you lock your house before you came to church? Because you believe in sin—there is larceny in the hearts of people everywhere. Why is there a lock on the ignition of your automobile? Certainly the car-makers in Detroit have no particular theological creed about sin; they just believe in sin from experience in a world full of car thieves! The uniformed policeman on the street corner is mute evidence of the reality of sin. The mounting cost of crime in our civilized society testifies to the battle we wage against sin. A bonded employee at the bank deposits your money in a vault behind a 12-inch steel case door, locked with an automatic time device—all because clerks and bankers as well as cutthroats and thieves have sin in their hearts.

When you applied for a credit card, you answered all kinds

of embarrassing questions about your debts and income, gave references about your character, and even signed a statement that you would pay your honest debts. Somebody suspected that even you might have a little of the sin of larceny in your own heart.

So the Bible says that sin is a *universal* reality. Sin has universally infected the heart of every man! The Bible says, "All have sinned and come short of the glory of God" (Rom. 3:23). This does not mean that all have committed *all sin possible* and are equally sinful. But *all* have committed *some* sin and have fallen short of God's perfection. All are not equally sinful but all are equally lost!

Imagine that we went together to the ballgame. The admission price is $1.00. I have only 35 cents and am far short and must stand aside. You have 99 cents, short only by one cent. But you are still short of the full price of admission and must stand aside with me. We are not equally short, but we are equally shut out. So some are short by only a bit of sin—others short because of much sin—but the Bible says all have sinned, so all are short of the glory of God, and all are lost!

The Nature of Sin

Then let us look to the Bible to see what God says about the nature of sin. Page after page catalogs the overt sins of the human flesh, lying, cheating, stealing, profanity, idolatry, drunkenness, adultery!

But sin is more than acts of immorality, or the breaking of the Ten Commandments! There is sin in the gutter! But there is also sin in a fur coat and a silk dress sitting on a church pew. There can be sin in righteousness and piosity, and even sin in prayer and worship. There is sin in the deed and there is sin in the heart. We discover that sin can be something other than an overt act. It may be an attitude, a spirit, a set of the mind and will.

The Old Testament uses three different Hebrew words for

sin—one meaning *missing the mark*, another *crookedness*, and yet another meaning *rebelling against authority*. In the New Testament four similar Greek words are used.

So sin is like an archer aiming the arrow and drawing the bow—but he misses the target. Man is made in the image of God for fellowship with God. He aims his life toward this high ideal—and misses! And with this failure comes depression, remorse, loneliness, and alienation. Sin is that which causes us to *miss the mark* in life and be lost from the purpose for which God created us!

Sin is *crookedness*, or "being twisted" which describes what sin does to us. As you would take a piece of paper between your fingers and twist it until it is broken, so sin takes the divine creation of man's body and spirit to twist it, and misshape it, and destroy it.

The gifted Rembrandt painted two portraits of himself. The first, early in life, shows him standing forth a handsome youth. The lamp of love burns in his eyes. His face shines like an alabaster vase with the genius and imagination that will beautify the world. The second portrait was painted twenty years later. During this time Rembrandt determined to deny himself no pleasure. He sought out every delight. He became a libertine. He betrayed his own self, lost faith in others, and forsook all faith in God. And we see the artist, shrunken, an old rag around his throat, weakness in his chin, the mark of the beast upon his brow, the eyes dull and without vision. The Bible says that this is what sin does—it twists and destroys every genius and faculty and capacity of human nature for beauty and achievement and goodness.

Sin twists and thwarts every honorable decent impulse of man. It points him in the wrong direction and turns him from God and right and love and brotherhood. Sin turns man's finest endeavors into failure. Sin has so twisted man that even while mankind escalates higher and higher intellecutally, scientifically, and culturally, man degenerates and sinks lower morally and spiritually.

1. Consider our *scientific advancement.* The technology of rocketry put a man on the moon. We called it "one small step for man—one giant leap for mankind." But this same technology also gave us the intercontinental ballistic missiles—armed nuclear warheads stockpiled in the arsenals of the world in sufficient quantity to destroy all living things on earth twelve times over!

2. Or consider our advances in *education.* It was only a century ago in Boston that the great dreamer Horace Mann launched the movement for mass education. Men believed that crime was due to ignorance. And mass education would eradicate crime in society! Today we have achieved and even surpassed the educational dream of Horace Mann—and crime has proliferated! Combine *all* that we spend on education, all that we spend on charities, all that we spend on churches—and the sum total does not equal the annual crime bill in the United States! We have discovered that the educated mind is not a changed mind—but simply more crafty and sophisticated in its tendency to evil and sin.

3. Or consider our *sociological advances.* A visionary political leadership launched a magnificent humanitarian "war on poverty"—a great society dream to match the resources of the affluent with the crushing human needs of Appalachia, the big city slums, the minority racial groups. Skilled social planners fed millions of Federal dollars into the program. But when the money began to flow, from the most idealistic social planner to the bureaucrat, and on down to the last political appointee in the program, forces of greed and self-interests took over in the hearts of the people involved. And by the time the tax money had filtered down to the poverty-stricken in the community, there was little left to give direct help to the poor! Sin twists even the highest ideals of unregenerate man and perverts his noblest purposes!

But the most revealing definition of sin is *"rebellion against God."* This is the root sin, the fundamental sin, the sin that strikes at the very heart of God and alienates us from him. All other expressions of sin would seem to be but fruits of the tree of which this rebellion against God is the taproot. The New Testament says that "the carnal mind is enmity against God" (Rom. 8:7). We are at war with God.

But you declare, "I'm not God's enemy! I have not declared war on God!" The Bible says that we are in rebellion against God when we refuse to acknowledge the authority of God over our lives. This was the basic sin of Adam and Eve; not the literal legal breach of the commandment, "Thou shalt not eat of the fruit of this tree," but the rebellion which said, "God says not to eat . . . but I will do *as I please,* not as God has commanded!"

So the basic sin that separates us from God is not some overt act, some particular dark deed, some evil habit that grips you. These are but the fruits of that basic sin which says, "My life is my own to live it as I please!" A young person excused the folly of another saying, "He is twenty-one years old and has the *right* to mess up his life if he *wants* to!" So we assert our *rights*—the *right* to have fun, the *right* to satisfy our desires, the *right* to determine our own destinies. We say, "It is *my* life, *my* business, *my* money, *my* family, *my* decision."

Sin is spelled "s-I-n." The middle letter is "I." It is a capital letter because "I" is the big thing in sin! "I" is central in sin. That egocentric assertion of "I" over the authority and will of God is rebellion against God. It is the essence of all sin which says, "I will not belong to God; I will keep my life for myself."

The Wages of Sin

The Bible says, "The wages of sin is death" (Rom. 6:23). In the passing of the generations of men, God has not changed his mind about sin. The effect of sin on the human race is still the same as it was in the beginning when God said, "The soul that sinneth, it shall die" (Ezek. 18:4). What is meant by death?

Sin has a deadly effect on the *psychic wholeness* of man. Sin brings life into conflict that splits us in two inside. A woman said to me, "I am all torn up." She meant that a battle was raging inside her. Paul cried, "The thing I would do, I do not—the things I do, I would not" (Rom. 7:15-16), as he described the conflict within him.

You have seen the circus bareback rider standing astride two horses as they pranced side by side around the ring. Have you ever wondered what would happen if one horse wheeled and started in the other direction? That is exactly what happens to us in sin. We are trying to ride two horses going in opposite directions. We are made of the dust and the flesh, with animal instincts coursing every fiber. But we have a second nature, the latent image of God in us. And there is a constant conflict and struggle between the two.

Walt Whitman pictured a contented cow in the field and asked, "Why am I not as the cow? It is not troubled with doubts and fears. It is not hopeless. It is not always whining about its sins, but seems content." And he goes on to paint an idyllic picture of the happiness he would have if he were a cow chewing the cud in the field.

But the answer is very simple; we are made in the image of God, by God for fellowship with God. And our souls are never at rest until we find him. And this inner conflict, between the nature of sin pulling in one direction and the image of God pulling in the opposite direction, literally destroys and makes dead our psychic being—unless we are delivered from sin by the power of God! That is why Jesus said, "No man can serve two masters" (Matt. 6:24).The soul that sinneth it shall sicken and die in its *psychic being.*

Sin brings death to the *conscience* of man. Implanted in man's nature is a God-given light that helps the human spirit distinguish between right and wrong, good and evil, the godly and satanic. Sin soon snuffs out that light, warps the judgment of man and brings death to the conscience of man.

Sin enables me to sit down with myself and talk to myself.

And in thirty minutes I can convince myself that anything I want to do is right! Psychologists call this "rationalization." But it is sin that causes us to lose our objectivity. So the serpent said to Eve, "God is cheating you. God is withholding from you something to which you are entitled. You have a right to eat the apple." Sin brought death to the conscience of Eve until she was able to openly disobey God and believe it was right! Truly the soul that sinneth, its *conscience* shall surely die!

Finally, sin brings *physical death*, *spiritual death*, and *eternal death*. You can be spiritually dead and still be very much alive physically. You can be dead spiritually right now, before the undertaker ever pumps embalming fluid into your veins. You can be spiritually dead and totally unconscious of the spiritual world about you. And if we are spiritually dead when physical death comes to us, we face the ultimate of eternal death.

Some people get terribly mixed up about heaven and hell, arguing over the reality and the nature of these two destinies. But fundamentally, hell is the continuation of that life which you have had on earth. If you have a life *without God*—separated from him—then you will be eternally separated from God. If you are *lost here* on earth, and pass over that line of death into eternity, you are *eternally lost!* And that is the worst kind of hell, surpassing even the most excruciating agony that the human mind can conceive, such as being burned alive, yet never able to die! And heaven is the promise of a life lived eternally *with God*, in his presence and in the fullness of his abundant eternal life.

So there is a basic flaw in the human spirit and in the fundamental structure of society. There is a demon inside every one of us! This evil power seems to be ingrained in the very dust of the earth. It seems to be passed from generation to generation as an incurable disease. We may call it sin, or by any other name. But changing the label on a bottle of carbolic acid and calling it "maple syrup" does not change the poisonous nature of the contents. *The soul that sinneth, it shall die!*

Deliverance from Sin

If death is the consequence of sin, how may we be delivered from sin?

You cannot bury a life of sin in a grave of forgetfulness and be delivered from it. You may use all kinds of psychological therapy to come to grips with your guilt complexes. But in and of ourselves we cannot deliver ourselves from our sins. Sin must be dealt with by God. He alone can cure the disease.

The Bible has been called a three-chapter story about sin. As we have seen, the first chapter tells of the *inception* of sin. Here in Adam and Eve we have a graphic account of how sin came into the world. Here we have the most profound and philosophically satisfying explanation of the origin and nature of evil man has ever known!

The second chapter tells of the *conquering march* of sin. From this tiny seed in the heart of man as he rebels against the authority of God by breaking one commandment, sin grows. We see it issuing in murder, lust, jealousy, hatred, until at last it consumes a world and all in it.

The third chapter is the story of the *defeat* of sin. It is climaxed by the wondrous story of how God became flesh and dwelt among us to defeat sin and deliver us from evil. He entered as Bethlehem's babe, died on the cross as the sinless Savior, entered the grave the full victim of sin, and came forth three days later victorious and triumphant over sin.

The Bible promises, "If we confess our sins, he is faithful and just to forgive us our sins, and to cleanse us from all unrighteousness" (1 John 1:9). I can no more confess your sins for you than I can die for you. You have sinned personally against God. You have rebelled personally against God. It is a personal matter between you and God. And you must deal personally with God in *confession* even as God has dealt personally with you when

Christ died for your sins on the cross. But if you believe this is the word of God and his promise is true, then get on your knees, confess your sins to God, ask him to forgive you through Jesus Christ. And he will deliver you from sin and give you life.

III

The First Step to God

Psalm 51:1-10

He sat with head downcast, fingers clenched, tears rolling down his face. He pleaded, "I want to get right with God. Tell me, what must I *do first*?"

The Bible says our first step toward God is to *repent.* Repentance is a word not often heard except perhaps in jest or levity. A television comedian regales his audience with a humorous punch-line in the dialect of a southern Negro preacher, "Now all you sinners gotta repent!" The newspaper cartoonist caricatures the minister as a skinny long-faced man in a stovepipe hat and tattered frock coat carrying a sign saying, "Repent—the end in near."

Repentance is not some verbal gimmick coined by a tent evangelist of yesterday. Repentance is not some abstract concept of a theologian in an ivory-towered classroom. Repentance is at the very heart and core of the gospel. It is a central theme of the Bible. "Repent" is the clarion call of the Old Testament prophet! "Repent" is the introductory theme of the New Testament. A strange man called John the Baptist, dressed in sackcloth and animal skin, comes out of the desert to preach and baptize in the Jordan River. Great crowds come down from Jerusalem to hear him. His message is one of hell, fire, and damnation as he declares, "Repent ye: for the kingdom of heaven is at hand" (Matt. 3:1-2).

Jesus begins his ministry in Galilee saying, "The time is fulfilled, and the kingdom of God is at hand: repent ye and believe the gospel" (Mark 1:15). Peter preaches at Pentecost. There is a great outpouring of the Holy Spirit and the people are amazed at the demonstration of the power of God. They cry out in conviction, "What shall we do?" And Peter answers, "Repent ye . . . in the name of Jesus Christ" (Acts 2:37-38).

Paul preaches to the intelligentsia of Athens on Mars' Hill. He speaks to the philosophers of creation and the unknown God and of philosophy and then tells these intellectuals that God "now commandeth all men everywhere to repent" (Acts 17:30).

So repentance saturates the Old Testament, permeates the New Testament and is a central theme of the gospel of Christ! What does repentance mean?

Mistaken Ideas

We have some strange ideas about repentance.

Some people think repentance is merely *being sorry* for sin. Of course, sorrow and remorse are elements in repentance. I read of a murderer on his way to be executed in the electric chair saying to his guards, "Stand aside and let my soul go to hell." Obviously he showed no remorse or sorrow for sin and for him repentance was impossible. But if I were to visit his comrades in the cell blocks asking, "Are you sorry?" I am sure most would say, "Of course, I am sorry; sorry that I botched the robbery; sorry that I got caught; sorry that I am being punished. Do you think I *like* to stay in jail?" Remorse is a starting point for repentance. But merely looking at our sins and its consequences with sorrow is not New Testament repentance.

Some people think that repentance is a kind of *currency* to bargain with God in order to escape the consequences of sin. An airplane was being pitched about in a violent storm. One terrified passenger prayed loudly unto the Lord, "O God, forgive me and save me and deliver me safely back to earth. I will give you half of all I own!" Finally the plane made it through the storm. As the man was deplaning, his seatmate took his arm and said, "I am a minister. I was so glad to hear your prayer. Now that you are down safely, I am sure you are ready to keep your promise and give God half of what you own." The man said, "Oh, no! I just now made the Lord a better deal. I promised to give God *all* I own if I ever get in another airplane." So some people think that repentance is what you do when you are in a heap of trouble. Just get on your knees and make a lot of promises to God and tell him you are sorry and he will get you out of trouble.

Some people believe that repentance is merely *acknowledging* the fact of sin. While conviction of sin is a necessary element, merely *being convicted* is not enough. It is one thing to be awakened at five A.M. by the alarm clock. It is another thing to get out of bed. It is one thing to be awakened, sensitive and conscious of our sins. It is another thing to move into action and do something about sin.

The *biblical meaning* of repentance is revealed in the very nature of the Greek word itself which means *turning around.* A learned theologian was holding a revival in a country church. One night he preached on repentance. He talked about the philosophical aspects, the grammatical context of the Greek word, and the theological implications of repentance. But the simple country people were unable to understand him.

Suddenly an unlearned country preacher started down the aisle waving his arms and shouting, "I am going to hell! I am going to hell!" Everyone thought he had gone berserk! When he reached the front, he spun around and marched back up the aisle shouting, "Now, I am going to heaven! I am going to heaven!" Then turning to the congregation he said, "That is repentance! To turn around. To go in an opposite direction. To turn from sin to righteousness, from Satan to God, from hell to heaven."

Repentance is a *turning around* in life. Repentance is something that can happen to you right now. When you repent, you can go forth with your feet traveling in the opposite direction, toward a different goal, walking in a different life, with a different commitment, with a different motivation, toward a different destiny. And the difference is as opposite as day and night, heaven and hell. It is a turnaround of 180°. No wonder Paul declared that the result of repentance was an entirely "new creation."

An Example of Repentance

But definitions are abstract. An example is worth ten thousand words. Here in Psalm 51 is a living example of repentance. This is the prayer of King David, a man who had sinned grievously. He committed murder and adultery. He had sinned against himself, against others, against God. One day, in great despair and sorrow, he examined his life, fell before God, and repented. Out of this repentance came a new faith, a new assurance of God's forgiveness and acceptance, a new life and a new relationship with God. David wrote of this wondrous experience in a beautiful song, this psalm. So here we have a living example of true repentance. Repentance and God's grace are mixed in the crucible of human experience to give redemption and deliverance. What then is repentance?

An Honest Look at Our Sins

If we are to repent, we must first see our sins as they are! So David sees his sin in all its ugly reality.

1. He said, "I have sinned" and missed the mark (v. 4). He remembers lying on his couch lusting and longing for the beautiful Bathsheba who belonged to another man. Wanting her more than anything else in life, the king arranged for her husband to be murdered and he took the widow for wife. But the wine of joy and fulfillment soon turns to ashes in his mouth. And he cries out, "I have missed the mark. God, you made me for higher things than murder and adultery and sin. How miserably I have missed the mark."

2. He said, "I have sinned," and my life is so *crooked* compared

to your righteousness. He pictures a farmer who has built a wall. He proudly looks at his handiwork and says, "That's a good wall—the straightest wall in the village." Others come by and praise him, "You are a good builder." Then the carpenter comes with the plumbline. He drops the string and the weight alongside the wall and reveals it to be crooked! So the king was full of righteousness and self-pride. He felt as we often do—I am the Lord's man! I give to his cause. I serve in his church. I am an exemplary father. I am a moral businessman. I am straight! Straight! Straight! but one day God puts his plumbline alongside. And when we are measured by God's standard we cry out with David, "I am not straight; I am crooked!"

3. David confesses that he is a *rebel* against God (v. 4). Now David was not a political or social or religious rebel. He pictures his broken relationship with God in domestic terms. It is the picture of two people who belong together, such as brother and brother, or father and son, or husband and wife. But the two who belong together have been separated and alienated from each other by the sin of one. I heard of a magnificent mansion on a huge estate in Canada occupied by a man and his wife. But they lived in opposite wings, never seeing each other, or speaking, separated by a wall of hate. So David feels the tragic separation. "My sin has separated me from God and made me a rebel." And the deepest longing of David's hungry heart is to be restored and reconciled to fellowship with the God to whom he belongs.

So if repentance is to truly transform your life and mine, we must take an honest look at our sin to see what it has done to us and to our relationship with the living God.

An Honest Acceptance of Responsibility

Second, we must honestly accept *personal responsibility* for our sins. This is very hard for us to do because our Adamic nature makes us natural "buck-passers." When God confronted Adam with his sin, Adam answered, "It is not *my* fault, Lord! *This woman* that *you gave* me made me do it." So Adam blamed his sin not only on Eve but on God himself for giving him a wife who would lead him astray. When God confronted Eve with her sin, she answered, "It is not *my* fault! The serpent that *you made* made me do it!"

So from Adam to this present generation we continue to "pass the buck" for the blame for sin. A couple with domestic problems comes to me for counsel. It is a familiar pattern. The husband says, "Yes, I did commit adultery, but my wife is not affectionate, and the girl in the office is a predator. I could not help it! It is not *my* fault!" The wife says, "Of course, I am cold and unresponsive. He makes me that way. And furthermore my parents never taught me how to show love and affection when I was growing up." So neither one accepts any responsibility for a failing marriage!

Heredity cripples us but does not make us *guilty* before God. *Environment* shapes us, but does not make us *innocent* before God. We are born of bad seed into a bad world. But the utlimate truth is that our *will* determines our sin. We sin because we choose to sin. And you will never know the full redeeming power of God and the full reward of repentance as long as you try to blame something or somebody else for your sins. You may blame your mate, your parents, the tensions of your work, the weak tendency within you, the hypocrites of the church, any of a score of various scapegoats; but you will never know redemption from your sins and peace with God until you come as did David saying, "It is *my* sin, *my* iniquity, *my* transgressions. *I* did it. *I* am responsible. *I* am wrong" (v. 3).

The Fruits of Repentance

Then David unfolds the gloriously wonderful things that happen when we come in true repentance to God. Isn't it strange, the one we sin against is the one to whom we turn when we really repent! We sin *against* God; then we turn *to him* in repentance.

David uses three beautiful pictures to portray what God will do for the penitent.

"Lord, I have sinned. But I pray, *blot out* my transgressions" (v. 1). Blot out means to *erase—erase* my sin. One Christmas we gave our children a "magic slate," a gadget of black cardboard covered with a plastic sheet. You would write and draw on the plastic surface with a wooden pencil. Then you could pull up the plastic sheet and, pop, all the marks disappeared. This magic slate kept the children entertained for hours. They would scribble and draw and then—pop—it was all clean and ready to start over again. Wouldn't it be wonderful if we could do that with life!

I get up in a bad mood in the morning and start the day all wrong. I am cross with my wife at the breakfast table. I get to the office and get in conflict with others. The day passes and I keep getting hostile, and short-tempered. And as I come home, I think, "What a mess I've made of my day! I wish I could make it go 'pop' and it all would disappear. I could start clean again."

But you know I cannot do that! No, I cannot; but *God can!* That is the promise of God when we repent. David says, "Cleanse me." Erase my sins! Take them all away! Ask him to give you a new start, to blot out your sins, and he will erase them!

The second picture: "Oh, God, *wash me* thoroughly from mine iniquity" (v. 2). *Wash me* is a laundry term. But it is not the automatic laundry down the street where you take your clothes, put them in a machine, drop in a quarter, pour in a cupful of high-powered detergent and your laundry is made "whiter than white" while you sit and watch television until the buzzer sounds.

When David was a shepherd boy tending sheep, he rescued a lamb from a thorn thicket. As he carried the lamb on his shoulders back to the flock, some blood from its thorn-torn side soaked the new tunic that David's mother had just woven for him. David did not know to soak the bloodstain immediately in cold water. He was ashamed when he took the garment to his mother that night. But his mother told him she knew how to remove the stain. The next day she went to the streamside laundry. She had no detergent or machine. She did as I have seen women around the world in Africa, Asia, South America do. She soaked the stained garment in water and then placed it on a rock and beat the cloth with a stick. She rubbed sand into the spot and beat it some more. She rinsed and beat and rubbed until every spot of stain was gone and it was clean again. And she gave the garment back to the shepherd boy all clean and new again.

So David says, "Lord, take this life of mine and wash it—just like that. Get everything out of it that is wrong, until I am white as snow." And that is exactly what God promises he will do for you and for me when we come in true repentance. He will wash us and make us clean.

The third picture: "*Cleanse me*" (v. 2). This is a ceremonial term of the Temple. Cleanse me; pronounce me "clean." A wife notices a festering sore on the back of her husband's hand. He comments, "It's nothing; but it seems to be infected and it will not heal." She insists that he go to the rabbi.

The man explains, "Rabbi, I am sorry to bother you with such a little thing, but look at my hand. It won't get well." The rabbi looks for a moment, then calls his assistant. They both look at the man's hand. They look at each other with knowing eyes. As they turn and look again at the man, written on their faces is the verdict of death! The rabbi says one word, "Unclean." And the man dies inside! He cannot return home. He cannot return to work. He must live outside the city like an animal. Whenever other human beings come near, he must call out, "Unclean! Unclean! Unclean!" For he has become a leper. So David says, "My sins have made me a moral leper! I am unclean in the sight of God."

One day this leper meets a man, a Galilean, who touches him and makes him whole. Then Jesus says to the man, "Go, show yourself to the priest." He goes to the priest. The priest calls his assistant again. They look at the hand. They cannot believe their eyes! It is a miracle! The leprosy is gone. And with great joy the priest says, "I *declare you clean!* You may go home for you are cleansed."

David says, "Oh, God, that is what I want you to do for me. Declare me clean so I can live. So I can be right with you, right with others, right inside myself."

That is what I need! Isn't that what you need, too? For God to declare you clean so you can live!

This is what God wants to do for everyone of us today. He wants to *erase* our sin, *wash* us and make us white as snow, and *declare* us *clean.* And this he will do if we come in repentance to him.

Repentance and Faith

There is no discernible line between repentance and faith. It is as the two sides of a hand. It is repentance as we move toward God. It is faith as we believe that in love and grace God will receive us as we commit ourselves to him. So in repentance and faith we must commit ourselves to Jesus Christ as Lord, as Savior, as cleanser, as the restorer of a broken fellowship, as the one who can declare us clean and righteous before God the Father.

A sign on a business announced, "Under New Management." There was no material external alteration, no change in the outward appearance, yet the announcement declared that a new person was in charge, new policies would prevail, new methods and practices would be carried out. That is exactly what repentance means in our lives! With Christ in our lives, there is a new manager. The operation of our life will be different.

So repentance is not merely a word, it is an act of surrender and commitment. God has done something about our sins and we must respond by doing something also. Nothing less than a turning from sin and a turning to him in total commitment is the first step to God!

IV
Being Twice Born

John 3:1-18

I was a guest at a private worship service in Washington for the inauguration of President Lyndon B. Johnson. The President had invited Billy Graham to preach the sermon. The President and the men of national prominence, Supreme Court justices, cabinet members, governors, were all seated before a Baptist preacher to hear a gospel message.

Mr. Graham spoke of the great need for moral reform and a spiritual revival. He warned that the greatest threat to our nation was not an invasion of communism from without but moral decay from within. He challenged the President to match his call for a "great society" with leadership in a spiritual and moral revival.

Mr. Graham concluded with a story about the President's grandfather Baines who was a Baptist preacher and president of Baylor University. On the wall of Mr. Johnson's office was a yellow letter written by General Sam Houston to Preacher Baines. Preacher Baines had won the wicked Sam Houston to Jesus Christ and had baptized him. Someone said to Sam Houston, "Well, General, I hear you were baptized and all your sins were washed away." Sam Houston replied, "If they were, then may the Lord help the fish down below!"

A Mandate from God

As Billy Graham told of the conversion experience of Sam Houston he emphasized the necessity of *every man* being transformed by Jesus Christ through a personal conversion experience.

Then he said, "Gentlemen, you have a higher mandate than that of the ballot box." To the President of the United States and to the nation's great assembled there he said, "You have a mandate from God!"

This is God's mandate to every person, *"Ye must be born again!"* Whether a President, or a nameless nobody, rich or poor, great or obscure, the mandate of God is the same, "Ye must be *born again.*" You cannot know abundant life here or eternal life hereafter unless you are *born again.* You cannot build a kingdom of God on earth or inherit the kingdom of God in heaven unless you are *born again.*

It is said that John Wesley preached more than 300 sermons on this text, "Ye must be born again." Someone said, "Why do you preach on this text so often?" He answer was, "Because ye *must* be born again."

An Honest Question

You say, "How can this be? What does it mean to be born again?" That is exactly the same question that Nicodemus asked in the story in John 3.

Nicodemus was a great man in Israel. He was religious, moral, of good reputation, educated, a rabbi, a member of the Sanhedrin, the supreme court of the Jewish nation. If he came to join our church today, we would receive him by letter immediately, and make him chairman of the finance committee, a deacon, and a Sunday School teacher! To others Nicodemus appeared to have everything that a religious experience could give. But inside, he was a hungry-hearted man. Something was lacking. And he longed for a vital personal experience with the living God and the assurance of citizenship in the kingdom of God. Nicodemus was a *lost* man!

So he came to Jesus by night, a *questing* man. Some would call him a coward, afraid to be seen with the master in the light of day. But I think more highly of Nicodemus than that. He sought

Jesus at night so as not to be pressed by the crowd. Nicodemus wanted to sit in leisure and talk at length with Jesus about the great issues of life. Perhaps his question went this way, "Surely thou art a teacher sent from God, for who could do these works except God be with him. Tell me, what must I do to be a child of God? To know in my heart I belong to God?" Jesus answered, "Ye must be born again or you will never see the kingdom of God."

Nicodemus was *confused!* "Born again? How can I reverse the process of life, re-enter and be born again from my mother's womb?" Jesus answered, "Marvel not that I said unto thee, Ye must be born again." Don't be confused, Nicodemus! I am not talking about physical birth. You were born once to become a physical being. You must be born a second time to become a spiritual being. "That which is born of the flesh is flesh; and that which is born of the Spirit is spirit." You must be born of *water* and the *spirit* to see the kingdom of God. "Water" does not mean water baptism! Jesus is striking a parallel. Physical birth is by water, as a doctor, or mother knows. If you are born only by water, physically, you are only a physical being. You must be born of the Spirit to become a child of God and a citizen of the kingdom of heaven. As there is a birthdate to mark the beginning of your physical life, you must be born again with a second birthdate to mark the beginning of your spiritual life.

Nicodemus' highly trained mind demanded a logical explanation. He was accustomed to a rational and intellectual explanation of life. He said, "It is difficult for me to accept anything I cannot explain or understand." Jesus said, "Nicodemus, you are a wise man. But that is a very foolish statement! You accept many things you cannot explain. See the breeze moving the leaves of the tree overhead? Where does it come from? Where does it go? You cannot explain the fact of the wind, but this does not keep you from experiencing its gentle touch on your cheek. Nicodemus, you do not reason your way to salvation. You take the leap of faith and experience it. *The validity of your faith is in the experiencing of it*—not in the *explaining* of it. Nicodemus, ye must be born again."

Regeneration Is Not . . .

What is this new birth mandated of us by Christ? Let me define it in negative terms, first.

The new birth, or *regeneration*, is not *generation!* In many other religions, generation and faith are linked together. A person born of Muslim parents is, by birth, a Muslim. A person born of Buddhist parents is, by birth, a Buddhist. A person born of Jewish parents is, by birth, a Jew. But a person born of Christian parents is not automatically a Christian by birth. The Christian faith of a father and mother does not make a child a Christian. In order for you to be saved, you must, as Jesus said, at some point beyond that first physical birth, have a second spiritual birth.

During a presidential election, one candiate, when asked if he were a Christian, answered, "Oh, yes! Although my parents were Jewish, they joined the Episcopal church before I was born!" I quite innocently created a furor when I publicly said that the candidate was confused—and was not a Christian. I was not casting reflection on his character or denying his qualifications for office. But I was challenging his theology and doctrine. For you cannot be *born* a Christian. You must be *reborn* a Christian. *Generation is not regeneration.*

Have you made this same tragic mistake? Have you assumed that because your parents were Christian, that because you were brought to the church from an early age, that because you have been reared in a Chrisitan culture, that makes you Christian! To you, even as to this good moral religious man Nicodemus, Jesus says that your physical birth into the church and into a religious family will not save you! Ye must be born again!

Regeneration is not *reformation.* A Christian is not merely a person who has cleaned up his life, reformed and straightened up. It is a worthy resolution to "turn over a new leaf and begin again." But to *reform* is not to be *born again*. Reformation means to drive down a stake today and say to God, "I am reforming and will live a perfect sinless life from this day on." But two things are wrong with this solution to sin. First, you *cannot* live a perfect life even though you try. Adam and Eve, in a perfect environment in the Garden of Eden, were not able to live above sin. Simon Peter walking constantly in the daily presence of Jesus Christ was not able to live above sin. And you or I, in our own strength, regardless of how firm our resolve to reform might be, cannot live a perfect life from now on, free from all sin.

Second, reformation does not take care of the debt for the sins of the past. For to begin now and sin no more (if you could) still leaves the guilt and condemnation of *past* sins resting upon us.

For example, suppose I unwisely ran up a bill of $10,000 at the department store, and I had no money to pay. So I go to the manager and say, "I will never do this again. From now on I will pay you cash for everything I buy!" The manager says, "That's fine, but what about these past debts?" But I would say, "Don't worry about the past debts. I have reformed and will not make any new debts!" Of course, you know that reforming does not absolve us of the debt of the past! There is only one way those past sins can be eradicated. They must be paid for. Jesus Christ died on the cross to pay that debt of sin. And only when you experience regeneration through him can you be delivered from the penalty and debt of past sin.

Baptism is not regeneration. How easy it is to associate the rites, the rituals, and the ordinances of the church with salvation until in our thinking they assume *saving power*. The devil causes our logic to slip and we permit the *symbol* to become the *reality*. And we are cursed then by trusting in the *forms* of religion to give us the *substance* of salvation.

Dr. Leo Eddleman was once a missionary to Israel. He tells

of preaching one day in an Israeli kibbutz filled with refugees fresh from the persecutions of Europe. One hostile listener challenged the Christian preacher saying, "Don't preach Jesus Christ, his love, and his brotherhood to us! If it is real, why don't you go and preach it to your Christian brothers, Hitler, Mussolini, and Stalin." The missionary answered, "They are not my Christian brothers." The refugee answered, "Oh, yes, they are! For Hitler and Mussolini were baptized into the Christian church as babies. And Joseph Stalin was baptized into the Russian Orthodox Church three times, face forward, by immersion before he was 24 months old. They were all baptized Christians! Go preach to them."

The missionary patiently explained, "Yes, these men belonged to a church tradition that believed baptism saves a person. But I am not here to preach that baptism and church ordinances and church rituals do not make one a Christian. To be a Christian, you must be *born again* through personal faith in Jesus Christ as Lord and Savior."

How this tragic heresy has blighted the churches of Europe and many of the churches of America. No ritual of water or bread, no rite performed by a man or church can make you a Christian. Yes, Hitler, Mussolini, and Stalin were baptized as babies but the water did not save them. And neither can we be saved by water, much or little! To be saved, you must be born again!

Neither is *church membership* regeneration.

Reformation does not produce regeneration—but I think regeneration should produce reformation.

Being baptized does not save you; but I think a saved person will want to be baptized to follow the example and the command of Christ.

Joining the church does not save you; but if you have been saved, you will love the church of the Lord Jesus Christ and desire to have fellowship with Christian brethren. I say this without malice but with firmness, "If some Christians do not love the Lord Jesus Christ any more than they love his church, they should go back and examine their hearts to see if they have really been saved!" Because, if you have been saved, you will want to be a member of the church bearing a testimony of Christ through the church.

Regeneration Is . . .

What *is* regeneration? Here are some positives:

Regeneration is a *personal experience.* It cannot be achieved by proxy. I can no more be saved for my child than I can die for my child. A Christian is a person who has made a voluntary, responsible personal choice by accepting Christ as Lord and Savior. In a personal way, *you* must respond to the grace and love of God in this commitment of your life to Christ.

Regeneration is a *mysterious experience.* We cannot completely explain it. It is by faith. As Jesus told Nicodemus about the wind, *experience, not explanation,* validates its reality. Who can explain love? We only experience it! But because we experience it, we know it is real. I cannot explain electricity, or television—but that does not prevent me from turning the switch and experiencing the benefits. So we must say, "Come into my heart, Lord Jesus," in faith. And he responds to that faith and comes in experience to us.

A bright student said to the pastor, "I have some questions to ask you about Jesus and the Bible. If you will answer these questions and satisfy me, then I will accept Christ." The wise pastor said, "Son, let me make you a proposition. You become a Christian first. Accept Christ as your personal Savior now. Then tomorrow, I will sit with you and answer every question." The boy agreed. He took the leap of faith and was saved. The next day the pastor said, "All right, let me hear your questions." The boy dropped his head and said, "It is a funny thing, pastor. But all my questions have disappeared or they seem so insignificant now. I have found Jesus Christ and he is so real, and I am so happy and satisfied in both my heart and mind that I guess I don't have any questions." That is regeneration—a mysterious but soul-satisfying experience.

Regeneration is a *transforming* experience. Regeneration changes us, our nature, our desires, our direction, our purpose. A man despairingly told his friend, "I just cannot get my life straightened out. I have been in and out of jail, drifted from one job to another, wrecked my home, broken the hearts of my parents. I wish I could run away to South America and start a new life all over again, a stranger beginning again in a brand-new world.

The friend counseled, "That would not do you any good. Because the first person you would meet on the streets of that new world would be your same old sinful self! And there would be the same old temptations, the same old problems, the same old sins, the same old difficulties. My friend, you do not need the world *around* you changed; you need the world *inside* you changed! And only Jesus can change that world inside you." "Will he do that?" the man asked wistfully. The friend said, "Yes, if you will ask him." And the slave of sin knelt and earnestly prayed, "Lord, change me!" And he was born again, transformed, made a new man with a new heart, a new nature. The Bible says, "If any man be in Christ, he is a new creature: old things are passed away; behold, all things are become new" (2 Cor. 5:17).

Regeneration is a *definite* experience. If I were to ask you, "Are you married?" You certainly would not say, "I hope I am!" Or, "Sometimes I think I am and sometimes I think I am not." Or, "At least I am striving and trying to be married!" You would answer either no or yes and point to a definite time and place when you stood in the presence of a minister and God and said your vows. At a definite time and place you made your commitment, you were married, and you established that union and relationship called marriage. Can you name the time and place when you were saved? When you made your personal commitment to Jesus Christ? When you invited him into your heart and you were saved? Regeneration is a definite experience! At a definite time and place one is *born again!*

Or perhaps you had such an experience many years ago. Now you question the genuineness of it. Again, using the analogy of marriage, there was one time when you were married but there have been many *renewals* of your vows, many recommitments to each other, many rededications to the ideals of marriage since then.

So in the Christian life, many times we fall short of the ideal and must come to *renew* our covenant with Christ. In this case it is not *regeneration* again, that we need, but *renewal.*

Perhaps you are still a baby Christian. You need to grow! Perhaps, as in marriage, you are still in an immature relationship and you need to grow to maturity in the Christian life. Regeneration is a definite experience. Some need to be born again. Others need to reconfirm that rebirth and renew their commitment to God.

How to Be Born Again

Then, you ask, "*How* may I be born again?" John writes, "As Moses lifted up the serpent in the wilderness, even so must the Son of man be lifted up" (John 3:14). You will recall that this is a reference to an experience of the children of Israel while they were in the wilderness. Many were sick and dying. A bronze serpent was lifted on a pole and the people were commanded by God to "look and be saved." When they responded in obedience and faith to God, they received life and healing.

That miracle of salvation prefigured Jesus Christ, lifted on the cross as the Savior for mankind afflicted by the sickness of sin. In like manner all who look to him, and believe on him, as the Savior lifted on the cross and dying for sin, shall not perish but have everlasting life. We cannot explain how God accomplished this any more than how God miraculously saved the children of Israel in Moses' day. But we *know* that God rewards obedience and faith with deliverance and healing and life.

Recently I flew in one of the huge new jet airplanes. I stood on the runway looking up at the monstrous tail towering several stories above me. The fuselage stretched out longer than a football field. I wondered, "How in the world can this monstrous thing fly!" It seemed absolutely inconceivable and impossible. It was beyond my comprehension and understanding. But I did not hesitate one moment. In fact, I was anxious to get aboard, settle down in the luxury of a cushioned seat, and relax in perfect faith and trust that the plane would fly and carry me to my destination across the ocean. Needless to say, it did!

I stand before the cross of Jesus Christ. It is beyond all my comprehension and understanding why God should so love me and Christ should die for me. I am so unworthy and he is so righteous. How did he manage to become God in the flesh and do this for me? How is the righteousness of God satisfied with the substitute that he makes with his own blood on the cross? How can the shedding of *his blood* accomplish the remission of *my sins?* These things I do not know. But this I know, I *am* a sinner. He *died* for *me.* When I confess my sins to him and believe upon him as my Lord and Savior, he saves me! In that experience, "I am born again." To you also, Jesus says, "*Ye* must be born again."

V

Good News for a Bad Woman

John 4:7-30

Traveling north from Jerusalem to Galilee one comes to the Arab town of Nablus. It nestles in a narrow valley between two mountains. To the left is Mount Gerizim where the Samaritans built their temple. Today a small colony of these biblical people, about 300 Samaritans, still lives here. They still worship at an altar on Mount Gerizim, offering blood sacrifices, accepting only the Pentateuch as the source of their scriptural authority, and awaiting a coming messiah. Opposite Mount Gerizim is Mount Ebal and on the slopes is the small village of Sychar.

At the edge of Nablus in the valley between the mountains is Jacob's well. Here Jacob watered his flocks and his herdsmen gathered to drink. Here today one finds the partially completed walls of an Orthodox church enclosing the site of the well. Two stairways lead down through 30 feet of debris to reach the ground level of Jesus' day. Here are the old curbstones forming a seven-foot circle enclosing the well. Here today the Orthodox priests will drop a bucket down to the water 65 feet below to bring forth a fresh cold drink from Jacob's well!

Jesus came to this very spot at midday to rest on the curbstone of the well while the disciples went into Sychar for food. Having traveled from Jerusalem, they were thirsty, hungry, and tired.

Contact

From the direction of Sychar comes a Samaritan woman with a waterpot on her head. She makes her way cautiously around the stranger seated here. She does not speak to him for this would be offensively inappropriate. But surprisingly, he speaks to her, equally as inappropriate, asking, "Give me to drink!"

Surprised by his forwardness, she answers, "How is it that you, a Jew, ask me, a *Samaritan* woman, for a drink? You Jews have nothing to do with Samaritans."

In 722 B.C. when the Assyrian conqueror Shalmaneser, took the Northern Kingdom of Israel, he carried the larger part of the Jewish population of Samaria into captivity. Foreign settlers from five eastern countries were imported to occupy this conquered territory. In the meantime, in captivity, ten of the twelve tribes were absorbed and lost in history.

When the remnant of two tribes returned later from the Babylonian captivity, they found the local Jews who had been left behind had intermarried with these foreign settlers. They called the resulting mixed-breed race *Samaritans* and despised them for compromising their racial and religious heritage. Hereafter the Jews had nothing to do with Samaritans. Jews would not eat from the same dishes that Samaritans used. Jews avoided traveling through Samaria. Samaritan was a dirty name! Jesus' enemies once said, "Thou art a Samaritan, and hast a devil" (John 8:48).

Not only was Jesus speaking to a despised Samaritan—but to a *woman*. Again, no self-respecting Jew spoke to a woman in public. A rabbi did not speak, even to his wife in public. Dr. Wescott, the Greek scholar, says that the devout Jew prayed daily in the synagogue, "I thank God that I have not been born a Samaritan, a dog, or a woman!"

Amazed, not only that Jesus would speak to her, a Samaritan and a woman, but also an *outcast* woman. For she had come alone at noonday to the well. In Jesus' day women did not appear in public alone. They came in groups. They came to the well early in the morning or in the cool of the evening. But it was obvious that this woman was an outcast. Other women would have nothing to do with her. So she came alone in the heat of the day to draw water to avoid the scorn of others.

Conversation

So she asked, "Why do you speak to me—a Samaritan—and a woman—unless . . . . " And I think she coyly cut her eyes at him . . . for she was probably a prostitute! Jesus answered, "If you knew who I am, you would ask me for a drink of living water." The woman laughed, "You have no bucket and the well is deep! And where would you get living water? Are you greater than our father Jacob who gave us this well?"

Jesus answered, "Whosoever drinketh of this water shall thirst again: but whosoever drinketh of the water that I shall give shall never thirst; but the water that I shall give him shall be in him as a well of water springing up into everlasting life" (v.14).

"Sir, give me this water, that I thirst not and neither come here to draw again," she wistfully replied. Quench the thirsting of my soul for identity, for purpose, for meaning, for significance! This is the universal longing of every heart in every generation!

Jesus said, "Go, call thy husband, and come hither." "But I have no husband," the woman replied. "Right! You have had five husbands! And the man you now live with is not your husband." She sounds like a Hollywood actress so often married that it was said she had a "wash and wear" bridal gown!

The Samaritan woman had flitted from one marriage to another and one husband to another, like a butterfly in a flower bed, seeking the sensual nectar of a new experience! Unbridled physical appetite had promised her satisfaction and excitement in infidelity. But after five empty marriages, with her latest man she had finally said, "What is the use of even going through the formality of marriage?"

Sin is like a drug: the more you take, the more you need; it never satisfies. A topnotch news analyst committed suicide. He left a note saying, "I am tired of running from one bar to another, from one woman to another, from one thrill to another, trying to fill 24 hours with frantic activity! I am so tired and fed up I am calling it quits!" The more we drink of the water of sin, the greater our thirst! But Jesus promised *living water!* Drink of this water and never thirst! The deepest longings and needs of the human heart are satisfied!

Confrontation

As Jesus confronts the Samaritan woman with her own problem saying, "I know—you have no husband—you are living in open sin with that man," her face must have flushed. Questions fly through her mind, "How does he know? Where did he learn of me? He seems to know who I am, what I have done, all about me!"

She quickly recovers her composure and asks a *diversionary* question, "I see that you are a prophet—a religious person! I have a question that has always bothered me about religion. My Samaritan ancestors have worshiped God here on Gerizim and they say that *here* is the house where God lives. But you Jews say that God lives in your temple on Mount Moriah in Jerusalem. Now tell me, where does God really live? Who is right, the Jew or the Samaritan?"

Hers was a *typical response.* When Jesus puts his finger on our sin, when he touches that sensitive spot in our lives, what do we do? Too many of us immediately react by trying to divert the conversation and evade confrontation with the real issue. We cover up by posing an intellectual or theological question: "All these denominations confuse me; which is really the true church?" Or, "I have never understood 'once saved, always saved.' Please explain that to me." Or, "What do you think about this new translation of the Bible?"

Early in my ministry I was pastor of a rural church. The hub of activity in that community was a crossroads general store. Here men would sit in cane-bottomed chairs on the porch, whittling and chewing tobacco, to argue politics, and religion. The owner of the store claimed to be an agnostic. He delighted in confounding the other men with unanswerable questions about religion and the Bible.

I became a close friend of the storekeeper and one day pressed him with the question, "Why don't you take the leap of faith and give your heart and life to Jesus Christ? No man knows the Bible better than you. No mind understands more clearly the claims of Christ and the issues involved! Why not open your heart in faith and ask Jesus Christ to come in as your Savior?"

He responded, "Preacher, I would! But there are so many unanswered questions in the Bible, so many things I do not understand. For example, where did Cain get his wife? That's not clear to me!"

I decided to use the strategy of Jesus in dealing with the Samaritan woman. I took a direct, open, frontal approach. I looked him straight in the eye and said, "You're right. It is not clear in the Bible where Cain got his wife. But, John, the Seventh Commandment is abundantly clear. 'Thou shalt not commit adultery.' You do understand that, don't you, John!" His ears turned red, his neck flushed, his face looked as if it would explode. For I had touched on what I knew, and others knew, and John knew was the *real* problem in his life. It was not Cain's wife that was bothering him; it was another man's wife. That was *his moral problem.* He jumped from his chair and stomped into the store. But a few weeks later John came to grips with his own moral problem, repented, and declared his faith in Jesus Christ!

Certainly, you have many questions about the Bible, the church, denominations, doctrine. But you understand enough to know that you have sinned against God, against others, against yourself. And you know enough to understand that God gave Jesus Christ on the cross as a Savior for your sin. And you know enough to understand that you must give an account to God for the response you make to the claims of Christ on your life. And as a Christian, it is clear to you what God expects in commitment, in Christian conduct, in service, in tithing, in love and loyalty to his church and his cause! The problem for most of us is not what we do *not understand* of the Bible and of our faith! Our problem is with what we *do understand* quite clearly, and choose to disregard!

Jesus answered the Samaritan woman, "God is not a physical person that lives in a physical house on Mount Gerizim or on Mount Moriah. God is spirit. And the time has now come when men shall worship him in spirit and truth. The sincere worshiper may open his heart and find God anywhere—and everywhere." The woman said, "I know that the Messiah is coming. And when he comes, he will tell us of all these things." Then Jesus said, "I am he, the Messiah, the one talking with you now."

The story ends with these words. No further conversation is recorded. Surely, there were more words spoken. But in the record we have only the essential outline of the incident.

Conversion

What happened? The Samaritan returned to the village of Sychar a converted woman! Jesus had given to her the living water that had changed her life! She went back home a new person, redeemed, transformed, made clean and whole again, the image of God restored in her, a scarlet heart washed and made white as snow! How do I know that the Samaritan prositute was converted?

First, I know she was saved *because of what she did*. She ran back to the village and left her waterpot sitting by the well. She was so excited and thrilled that she completely forgot the reason why she had come to the well in the first place. The forgotten empty waterpot at the well curb testifies that something wonderful happened to her when she met Jesus at the well.

Second, I know she was saved *by what she said*. The Samaritan woman ran into the village shouting, "Come, see a man who told me everything I have ever done." This was the worst possible thing she could have said! She was shouting in the streets, "Come out to the well; there is a man who knows all about me!" That is all the gossips of Sychar wanted, someone who could tell them *all* the sordid ugly things in the life of this notorious woman.

But the converted Samaritan woman was saying that here is one who *really* knows all about me, how dissatisfied and miserable and unclean I have felt inside, how I have longed for forgiveness and cleansing, how desperately I have wanted a chance to begin over again and make a new start in life! Even as Jesus knows each one of us as we *really* are—inside! He knows the nameless longings and the secret yearnings of your heart. He knows the deep desire within you to be decent and clean. He knows the remorse and the shame that you feel. He knows how desperately you want to be loosed from the shackles of habit that bind you. He knows you, not only at your worst in your sins, but at your best in your highest moments of worthy aspiration. This is the all knowing, all understanding, all loving Christ that wants to satisfy your thirst for the living water, also.

Third, I know she was saved *because of what Jesus did.* When the disciples returned with food, Jesus said, "I am no longer hungry. For I have food to eat that ye know not of." For Jesus had encountered life's most satisfying experience. He had shared the good news of God's love, forgiveness, and acceptance with a lost sinner. When somebody takes your hand and says, "Thank you for bringing me to Jesus—because of you, I have a new life, new home, a new hope, a new outlook, a new destiny"—truly that is life's most satisfying and rewarding experience!

Finally, I know she was saved *by the results!* The Bible says that many of the Samaritans in Sychar believed in Jesus because of the woman's testimony. She became the first woman evangelist recorded in the Scriptures as she ran into the village proclaiming the wonderful thing that had happened when she met Jesus!

Conclusion

Only the Gospel of John records this heartwarming story of

the conversion of the Samaritan woman. Why did he select this incident to preserve for us? I believe John wanted us to come to a firm conclusion and conviction about two things: first, the *universal need* of *all* persons to be saved; and second, the *universal salvation* that all may find in Jesus Christ!

In the third chapter, John tells of the conversion of Nicodemus: a Jew, a religious leader, a member of the Sanhedrin, a moral man, a religious man, an honorable and respected citizen, the finest flower of Judaism. Yet *he* was a lost man who needed Jesus and who found life eternal in him.

Then in this chapter immediately following, is this encounter of Jesus with a Samaritan: a woman, an outcast, a grossly immoral and wicked person. She, too, like Nicodemus, found a new birth, a new beginning, and life eternal in Jesus Christ. So John is saying that all persons, good and bad, moral and immoral, regardless of rank, race or religion, need Jesus!

Furthermore, John says, from the top to the bottom of society, no person is beyond the reach of the gospel or the transforming touch of Jesus.

So we have this certainty that any life can be made over, from Nicodemus to the Samaritan woman and all in between.

This is our assurance today that Jesus stands before you, as he stood at Jacob's well, offering to quench your spiritual thirst with living water. He stands as a *living* person, a present-tense reality, to give you forgiveness and cleansing. He wants to send you back into the daily routine of your life a changed person.

He is the same Jesus who met the Samaritan woman and knew all about her—even as he knows today who you are, why you are here, and what your heart's need is this very moment. If you will but ask him, he will fill your cup, today!

This is good news—for a bad woman—for a good woman! Good news for a bad man—or a good man! Good news for young and old alike! Good news to everyone! Jesus Christ promises to each of us forgiveness and cleansing and a life made over again in him.

VI

Saving Faith

Hebrews 10:38 to 11:6

The setting is a cold damp cell in a monastery in Germany early in the sixteenth century. A monk sits, day after day, night after night, contemplating the deeper meaning of six words written on the wall. He had felt guilt-ridden and longed for the assurance of God's forgiveness.

He had attempted in many ways to do penance for his sins. He had even made a pilgrimage to Rome and climbed the *Scala Sancta,* a stairway believed to have come from Pilate's hall. The monk had crawled on his knees up the steps, kissing each one and praying for forgiveness. Halfway to the top a voice seemed to speak the six words now written on the monastery wall: "The just shall live by faith."

The monk's name is Martin Luther. The verse on the wall is found first in Habakkuk and repeated three times in the New Testament in Romans, Galatians, and Hebrews.

"The just shall live by faith." These six words express the central core of Christianity. Here is the *Magna Carta* of religious liberty. Here is a spiritual *Declaration of Independence* for the human soul. Here is our religious *Constitution* and *Bill of Rights.*

These six words declare a man is made righteous, or found acceptable by God, not on the basis of his good deeds, or his creed, or his acts of penance however sincerely done, or his church relationship, or his racial or cultural heritage. A man is made righteous and acceptable to God by *faith! Personal* faith! *Responsible* faith! *Expressed* faith! Faith *affirmed* in the heart of the believer.

"The just shall live by faith." Thomas Carlyle said that a nation rises or falls according to its attitude toward Martin Luther and these six words. Affirmed in the Scriptures and validated in human experience, *faith* is God's open channel whereby we come to him to be saved and he comes to us in grace to bless and to heal and to strengthen.

The Definition of Faith

If faith is central in the Christian experience, what than is *saving New Testament* faith?

Faith is not as the little boy described, "Believing what ain't so." Yet some people believe that faith is a blind, uncritical belief contrary to fact, and contradicting reason. They conceive of faith in conflict with intellect, of faith and reason as adversaries.

The writer of Hebrews sees faith as the completion and fulfillment of reason. For example, consider an athlete making a broad jump. He races with all his might and power full speed down a cinder track to where the line is drawn for the jump. The cinder track is reason. So man pursues reason as far as he can go with all the vigor of his being. But finally the track runs out; he comes to a line where reason goes no further.

When the runner comes to the end of the cinder track, does he stop or draw back? Without hesitation and with all the momentum and power of his being the runner jumps into the air and leaves the track in one mighty leap! So Christian faith, rightly understood, is that leap we take after we have pursued reason to its end. Faith carries us beyond reason to the fulfillment and completion of the race of life. Instead of a *contradiction*, faith is the *completion* of reason that brings us into the full knowledge of life and its meaning.

The Possession of Faith

The writer of Hebrews defines faith as the "*substance* of things hoped for."

What is *substance?* The translators of the King James Version grappled with the true meaning of this Greek word. To them it was obscure. However, since that time archaeology and biblical studies have given us more light on the language of the New Testament. We have discovered thousands of *papyri,* paper fragments and documents, from the New Testament era written in the vernacular of that day. And in the papyri we find this word occurring many times. The word translated *substance* is used in a secular context in the papyri as a commercial term meaning a *title deed* to property.

You own property in Florida but you live in Kentucky. You cannot see your property or claim it by physical occupancy. Then how do you know you own it? You have a *title deed* that validates your ownership. So faith is the *title deed* of "things hoped for . . . of things not seen." Faith gives us a stake, a claim, a guarantee of possession in a world that we cannot see!

We live in two worlds. First there is the seen world which is obvious. It is the world measured by a 12-inch ruler—the world put on the scales and weighed—the world analyzed in the test tube and examined in the microscope and seen through the telescope—the world we see, feel, touch, hear—the physical world about us.

Some people want to believe that this "seen" physical world is the *only* world! But, there is a vast unseen world that is often a greater reality than the seen world. As residents of this unseen world we are continually influenced by it.

1. For example, there is the *relatively* unseen world of the *past.* Every day we live in its shadow and are shaped by it. Did you ever see Abraham Lincoln? Or hear George Washington speak? Did you attend the Continental Congress or the Constitutional Convention? Of course not; but the unseen world of yesterday's early America and its idealism and concepts of democracy continue to shape our destiny today!

2. There is the *relatively* unseen world of the *present*. Have you seen China? Eight hundred million communist Chinese? Mao Tse-tung? The oil sheiks of the Arab world? Yet your life and mine are daily being shaped by that vast unseen world of unseen people and faraway lands. It would be absurd to deny the reality of these unseen worlds!

Then there is the *absolute* unseen world that no one has ever seen, and never will. But it is a reality! Have you ever seen love? Influence? An idea? Communism? These are intangibles in an absolute unseen world that daily affect us.

3. The writer of Hebrews refers to another dimension of this unseen world—the unseen world of the *future*. We live today in that world also! That is why I have food stored in the freezer, money deposited in a savings account, and make payments on an insurance policy!

So I have made my point! Admittedly, there *are* two worlds—this seen physical world and a vast unseen world—and we live in both.

God has created man to live in both worlds. God has equipped us to live in a physical world. He made us physical beings with physical bodies, instincts, and capacities to get along in the seen world. God gave us hands to touch, eyes to see, ears to hear, bodies for living in, reason to examine and understand this physical world.

In like manner, God has uniquely equipped us to live in the unseen world. The writer of Hebrews says that the endowment or equipment for the unseen world is *faith!* Faith is the "title deed" to the possession of that world. Faith is the God-given spiritual instinct that enables us to live victoriously in this unseen world.

So the Bible says, "Faith is the *title deed* of things *hoped for*"—in the future. Faith is the tangible, concrete evidence of our possession of "things not seen." What a profound idea!

The Universality of Faith

"Well," you say, "I don't have any faith!" Not so! Not so! Not a living person can say, "I have no faith." *Everyone* has faith! And everyone must live by faith every day!

You stamped and mailed a letter yesterday. You dropped it in the mailbox and had faith that Uncle Sam would deliver the letter to its destination in California! Yet you have never seen *Uncle Sam*, and neither have I!

Or consider a more dramatic example. You are driving down the highway at 55 miles per hour. Hurtling toward you at the same speed is another driver only two feet to the left of a yellow line running down the middle of the road. Here are two massive two-ton deadly missiles hurtling at each other at a compounded speed of more than 100 miles per hour. If the driver of that other vehicle swerves only four feet over into your lane, it means instant death! Do you pull off the road until that car passes? Of course not! You have faith! First, faith in the operational *competency* of the unknown driver in that unknown car hurtling toward you. Then you have faith in the *rationality* of that person—that he will not act irrationally and deliberately swerve into your lane at the last second. Then you have faith in the *morality* of that person—that he does not want to kill you. So every time you face and pass a car on the highway you are exercising great faith! It is impossible to live without faith—an abundance of faith—every day!

The Object of Faith

Our problem is not the *lack* of faith, or a weakness of faith. The issue is the *object* of faith. This is the crux of the matter.

Today we have faith in all kinds of things. We say, I have faith in *myself*—my own ability to make my own way in the world. Others may falter and fail—but not me. I will overcome."

We say, "I have faith in the unlimited capacity and ingenuity of the *human mind* and spirit to solve the social and economic crises of our day."

We say, "I have faith in *America!* The great democratic system of free enterprise will overcome and persevere."

We say, "I have faith in the great twentieth-century dream of *success*. If I can just be a success in life, then life will be rich and full and wonderful for me and for my family."

So the crux of the matter is not whether you have faith; the question is, "In *what* have you placed your faith?" What is the object of your faith?

E. Stanley Jones, the great Christian missionary to India, spent a long period in the hospital recuperating from a severe illness. The window of his room overlooked a deep gorge. As he looked out each day, his attention became fixed on a vine growing from his side of the ravine. Day by day he watched the growing vine stretch out toward the other side.

Dr. Jones said that he became obsessed with the struggle of the vine as it twisted and reached out trying to span the chasm. Every morning when he awakened he looked out the window to see if the vine was still there. One happy morning he saw that the vine had at last touched the far side and a tiny tentacle had laid hold on a large tree. He felt an emotional surge of victory in his own heart, as the vine had won its struggle and was finally tied on to the other side. In the weeks that followed it grew into a massive green bridge anchored firmly around the tree on the far side.

One night he was awakened by a violent storm. The wind blew, lightning flashed, rain beat against his window. He wondered anxiously, "What of the vine?" But he went back to sleep with the calm assurance that it was safely anchored to the mighty tree on the other side. But when daylight came he looked out and the vine was gone—swept into the ravine by the storm! He looked for the tree, the anchor on the other side. And he saw only a rotten stump. For the vine had tied itself to a rotten tree.

And when the storm came, the anchor gave way.

That is the oft-repeated tragedy of life. Too many of us have anchored our faith in the rotten stumps of this world. Our own abilities, our position, our race, our money! But every human resource is a rotten stump!

What is the only worthy stump that will hold as an anchor for faith in the storms of life?

You say, "Well, the object of my faith is the *Bible*. It is a lamp unto my feet, a light unto my path. It is the inspired Word of God, a worthy guide for faith and practice." Yes, that is all true. But the Bible is a rotten stump if it is the supreme object of your faith. For even the Word of God does not say, "The Bible was wounded for our transgressions—or that God was in the Bible reconciling the world unto himself." The Bible is the Word of God but it is not to be the object of our faith.

You say, "I can tell you *what* I believe. My *creed* is the object of my faith." We need a creed, a doctrine, a theology to give skeleton and structure to what we believe. But a creed is not to be the object of saving faith; it is a rotten stump.

You say, "I am counting on the *church* to save me." The church is the body of Christ in the world, but the church is not to be the object of saving faith. The church, too, is a rotten stump.

The supreme object of saving faith is the *person* of Jesus Christ. We must cut clean through to the central truth of Christianity as did Martin Luther. "The just are saved—made righteous before God—not by the Bible, not by the church, not by creed, not by ritual, not by penance, not by good works, but by faith in the person of Jesus Christ." He alone is the solid anchor or object for faith.

The Content of Faith

What is to be the *content* of faith? *What* am I to believe to undergird my faith?

First, I must have a basic belief about God. God is! God exists!

This affirmation is the north star that guides us. H. G. Wells said, "If there is no God, nothing matters. If there is a God, nothing else matters."

Second, I must believe this God who exists and who made us has spoken to us. A God that is dumb and does not speak is no God! A God that does not reach out to redeem his creation is no God.

Third, I must then believe that Jesus Christ is the revealed Son of God. Jesus is not merely a higher man, a greater teacher, a keener mind. He is God among us! When we accept this premise, we have no difficulty with the virgin birth, or the miracles, or the resurrection.

Fourth, I must believe that Jesus Christ died on the cross, not as a martyr for a lost cause, but as a substitute for my sins. In his body on the cross he took the penalty of sin for us. Through him we have forgiveness and deliverance from sin.

Fifth, I must believe in the resurrection. Paul said, "If there is no resurrection, our faith is in vain." Without the resurrection, death is the end. Sin is the victor. Satan still rules and reigns. But it is a glorious fact that on the third day Jesus came forth alive, resurrected forevermore. He is a living, victorious, present-tense Lord. This is the content of faith to be placed in the object of faith, Jesus Christ.

The Results of Faith

What happens when I exercise this kind of saving faith in Jesus Christ? The Bible says that we are *converted,* or "turned around." Our life is set in another direction. We have different goals, ideals, purposes, and a different destiny.

The Bible says we have a changed *relationship.* We are born again, a new creature. We have a changed *nature.* We have the nature of God in us to replace the old carnal nature of sin. We have a changed *identity.* Now are we the sons of God, a member of the heavenly family. We have a changed *destiny.* We have been turned from death to life, from hell to heaven.

The Exercise of Faith

How can we possess this kind of faith? You do not come into saving faith by majoring on your doubts. The Bible says, "The fool hath said in his heart, There is no God." That is the fool's way of starting at faith—to gather all his doubts in a basket and bring them to God saying, "Settle my doubts first. Then I will have faith."

You must reverse the procedure. Put doubts aside and start with faith. What *can* I believe? What *do* I believe? Start by living up to the highest understanding and measure of faith you already possess. You can say: I *can* believe in a *creative force* called God. I *can* believe that he is *rational* and *loving*. I *can* believe in a *moral order*. I *can* believe *right* is better than *wrong*. I *can* believe that *goodness* is better than *sin*. I *can* believe that this God wants to *save me*. Start with what you *can* believe. Run down the cinder track of reason saying, "I can—I can—I can." Finally, when you get to the end of reason and doubt has drawn a line, like the broad jumper, throw yourself with all your might into the air and take the leap of faith! And you will find that you will be saved by faith!

A young man was walking home with the evangelist from the morning revival services of a country church. The preacher said, "See that oak tree in the fence row? Imagine that you have climbed into the top branches and I was standing below. If I told you to jump and I would catch you, would you jump?" The boy dropped his head and said, "No, sir." "Why?" the evangelist asked. "I know you would try, but I do not know if you are strong enough to catch me," the young man said.

"Son, that is unbelief," the evangelist said. "But suppose Jesus Christ stood here. You knew he was the Son of God. You knew he had all power. You knew he raised the dead, healed the sick, stilled the storm, cured the blind, came up alive from the grave.

If Jesus stretched out his arms and said, 'Jump,' would you?" the evangelist asked. The boy thought a moment and said, "Yes." "Why?" the evangelist asked. "Because I believe if Jesus said he would catch me, he could and would!" "*Son, that is faith!*" the evangelist replied.

That night the boy sat through the service. And when the invitation was given, he took the leap of faith and came forward, to receive Christ as his Savior. That day Jesus saved, by faith! He is now a preacher of the gospel!

In the same simple way you, too, must take the leap of faith to be saved.

VII

The Restless Eyes of God

2 Chronicles 16:9

I was in the cockpit of a private plane skimming a sea of billowing cotton-like clouds at 10,000 feet. The pilot, a young deacon named Dave Michael, was explaining the instruments on the panel.

"That is the radarscope," he said, and pointed to a glass screen on which a dark shadow swept back and forth like an automobile's windshield wiper. "There is the skyline of Louisville," he explained. "The radar sweeps the horizon sending out signals to pick up objects in our path." Then he reached for a leather-bound book on the instrument panel shelf and said, "This radar reminds me of a verse in my paraphrased *Living Bible*—a verse on which I have staked my life." He handed the Bible to me and said, "It is 2 Chronicles 16:9. Would you like to read it?"

I found the text and read aloud, *The eyes of the Lord search back and forth across the whole earth*—he interrupted, "Just as the radar is sweeping the horizon, God's eyes are sweeping the earth"—*looking for people whose hearts are perfect toward him*—again, he said, "God is sending signals throughout the whole world to all men everywhere to find those who will respond to him"—*so that he can show his great power in helping them!*

Dave said, "I really believe that! God is just looking for people he can trust. People who will commit themselves to him. He wants to help them! Let me tell you how God has helped me since I made that total commitment to him, since I committed my business, my family, my life, my all saying, 'Lord, it's all yours.'" Dave continued to tell me all the exciting wonderful blessings and joys that had come to him, even in times of testing and trial, because of this commitment.

As he talked, I read again that verse and wondered how in the world I had ever missed such a magnificent and almost unbelievable promise of God. Have you ever heard a more wonderful and unlimited promise? "The radar-like eyes of the eternal God sweep the earth ever looking for people who will commit themselves to him so he can demonstrate his power by helping them!"

The Occasion

When and where was it that God made this promise? It was more than 2,500 years ago. Asa was king of Judah. His enemies in adjoining countries were about to engulf the tiny nation, seizing cities and carrying off the people into captivity.

There was a mighty king of Syria named Ben-hadad with a great army more powerful than the enemies of Judah. But Ben-hadad had made an alliance with Asa's enemies. The king of Judah conceived a plan to deliver his nation. He gathered all the wealth of the palace and the temple, the gold, silver, and jewels. Then he sent a messenger to Ben-hadad saying, "If you will break the treaty with my enemies and come over to Judah's side, I will give you all this treasure." So Ben-hadad took the silver and gold and joined in an alliance with King Asa.

It was then that the prophet of God, Hanani, appeared before Asa and said, "O king, have you forgotten the Ethiopians? Have you forgotten the Lubims? When these people came against you, you trusted in God for deliverance. And they were defeated. But, now, you have forsaken God and you are trusting in an alliance with this pagan king to deliver you. Have you not learned that God is always looking, his eyes searching to and fro, to find a man he can trust so he can show his great power by helping him? Now, because you have trusted in your own wisdom instead of God, you will never again live in peace!"

So it was! Asa knew only war until he died, afflicted with a terrible sickness!

God has not changed his eternal purpose and will for mankind since the days of Asa! His restless eyes are still looking for men!

This is truly an amazing revelation! I once heard a man from India speak at a World Congress on Evangelism. He said, "We have many religions in our land! But without exception they all dwell on the question, 'How can man find God?' The people are all searching and questing for God! But the wonderful news of Christianity is 'How God has found us through Jesus Christ.' Instead of man looking for God, it is God looking for man."

All men have instinctive religious yearnings and longings. They inevitably seek after some infinite being or power outside and beyond themselves—the *great mind*, the *first cause*, the source of *life*, the Almighty *God!* But the good news of Christianity is that this God is searching for you. And this has been his endless quest from the foundations of the world.

That is the theme of the Bible! In the very first pages we read of Adam and Eve. Their sin separated them from God. Then God came looking for them in the garden and the first recorded words of the living God after man's fall were, "Adam, where art thou?"

On the very last page of the Bible we find the living God still engaged in this endless quest pleading, "And the Spirit and the bride say, Come. And let him that heareth say, Come. And let him that is athirst come. And whosoever will, let him take the water of life freely" (Rev. 22:17).

And in between these pages are the dramatic accounts of this persistent and loving God ever seeking men. He seeks out crooked and deceitful Jacob with an angel who wrestles him and will not let him go until Jacob is transformed into the new man, Israel. He seeks out a runaway Moses hiding in the Midian desert and through a burning bush calls him back to lead a nation out of bondage. He seeks David hiding in the hills of Judea and leads him back to unite a kingdom. He seeks Elijah cowering in a cave in despair and with a still small voice calls him to preach to the king. He seeks Jonah deep in the hold of a ship on the high seas, delivers him out of the belly of a great fish and sends him as an evangelist to the wicked city of Nineveh. He seeks a fiery young rabbi on the Damascus road and turns him from murder to the calling of a missionary. God's endless quest is summed up in Jesus Christ himself saying, "The Son of man is come to seek and to save that which was lost" (Luke 19:10).

Even so, God is looking for you, today, wherever you are!

His Many Ways

How is it that God seeks us?

He seeks us through his Word, the *Bible*. When we open this book, it becomes more than mere printer's ink on India paper, more than glue and cloth and leather binding. In a supernatural way, this, *his Word*, becomes a vehicle through which God speaks to us. As we read the Bible devotionally, it becomes a channel of communication from the living God to our heart.

In a Billy Graham crusade I was a platform guest with a three-star army general who gave his testimony. He said, "I drank like a fish, engaged in all kinds of immorality, practically wrecked my marriage and my career!" He continued, "Then one evening, all alone, I took an honest look at my life and realized how miserable it had been. I knew I needed God but I did not know how to be saved. I called my wife's pastor on the telephone and asked him what to do. He told me to read the third chapter of John and do what the Bible said."

The general continued. "As I read the third chapter of John, God spoke to me. I knelt beside my chair and said, 'I believe in Jesus as my Savior. Forgive me for my sins and I will live for Jesus.' That night changed my life! Today, I am a new man. My supreme desire in life now is to live for Jesus Christ!"

Recently, a seminary student told of his calling to the ministry. While a student at the University of Alabama, he was sitting in his dormitory window at midnight, looking out into the starry sky. He said, "I realized how empty and meaningless my life really was. I was floundering. I had no direction or purpose. I picked up the New Testament that my mother had given me and began to read. Then the pieces began to fall into place in my life as God spoke to me. I found his will for my life and I have entered the ministry." So God speaks to us, saved and sinner alike, through the Bible, his Word.

God seeks us through the myriad *events of life*, the tragedies, sorrows, crises, failures, disappointment, discouragements. A young matron said to me, "I have everything that anyone could want in life—a beautiful home, a wonderful husband, three lovely children, freedom from financial worry or care; yet I am absolutely bored and fed up with life. I am looking for something I don't have and these *things* cannot give me!" Thus Jesus was calling her through this heart hunger. And he found her and supplied her need for significance and meaning and worthwhileness in life.

God seeks us through the call of the *Holy Spirit*. Every longing and desire that you have to live right, to be free from your guilt and sin, to love and be loved by God—that is the calling of the Holy Spirit of God seeking you.

Ultimately, God seeks us through the very *cross of Calvary* itself. When we see the extremity to which the love of God has gone to seek us out and save us, we respond: "Love so amazing, so divine, demands my soul, my life, my all."

A missionary was showing colored slides on a bed sheet stretched on a mud wall in an African village. He threw on the screen a life-size picture of Calvary, showing Jesus in all his agony suffering and dying. As he told the story of how this sinless Son of God was crucified for sinners, an African native became so overwrought with the realism of the picture and the story that he ran forward crying, "Come down! Come down! I am the one that should be on that cross, not you, Jesus. For I am the sinner and deserve this death."

So the artist Rembrandt painted his own face on a Roman soldier standing by the cross! During the Second World War a Swiss artist painting the crucifixion scene showed the Roman soldiers wearing a Swiss army helmet! The artwork of a current religious magazine depicts the suffering Christ, crowned with thorns, and draped in an American flag! The legend below is "They crucified him." So we see Calvary and see ourselves, and God touches our heart to condemn us as the sinner who crucified Christ.

So God is in the world, endlessly seeking and searching for men, for every one of us, through many means and ways!

What Kind?

What kind of people is God looking for? The prophet says, "Those whose hearts are *perfect* toward him." You say, "Then, that lets me out! I am certainly not perfect!" On the other hand, if we were perfect, why would we need God?

The problem is in the word *perfect*. We generally understand perfect to mean "without flaw" or "sinless perfection." If God is only looking for men who have no sin in their lives, no wrongdoing, no guilt, of course, that excludes all of us! But this common understanding of the meaning of *perfect* is an inadequate expression of the original language of the Bible.

A better translation is "perfected, completed, fulfilled, or committed." Sometimes we ask, "Are your plans perfected?" We do not mean, "Are they without flaw, but are they completed or fulfilled." So, literally, God is looking for people who, like the radarscope, will fulfill, respond to, complete, and bounce back his signal. He sends out grace and wants it completed or fulfilled with faith. He sends out love and wants it to bounce back in commitment, consecration, surrender. God is engaged in an endless quest seeking men who will respond to him.

One of the masterpieces of Christian art is Holman Hunt's painting, *Jesus the Light of the World*. The original is in St. Paul's Cathedral in London. There, before you, larger than life itself, stands Jesus. Wearing regal robes, with lantern in hand, he stands before a closed door knocking. The door is covered with cobwebs and ivy, sealed by time and neglect. So the artist dramatizes the words of Jesus, "I am the light of the world" standing at the door of the human heart saying, "Behold, I stand at the door and knock." A closer examination of the picture reveals an apparent careless error on the part of the artist. Every detail is masterfully presented in the most faithful of colors except there is no knob or latch on the door!

But instead of an oversight, this omission is deliberate. The artist is visualizing an awesome truth. There is no latch on the outside of the door to a man's heart. The door can be opened only from the inside. When God made man, he determined that this distinctive of deity, this freedom of choice and will, this image of God in man would not be violated. God himself will not force open the door to a man's heart. Jesus Christ will not come as a house-breaker or univitied intruder. The Son of God stands outside, knocking waiting for the latch to be lifted on the inside.

So John, in Revelation 3:20, pictures Jesus as knocking at the door saying: "If you, on the inside, hear my voice, and if you will reach up and lift the latch on the inside and open the door to invite me in, I will come in and abide with you." That is exactly what the prophet Hanani said to Asa the king, "God is looking for men who will respond to his signal . . . and who will commit their lives to him in faith."

Why?

Why does God want men to respond to him? To make slaves of them? To exploit them? No! God is looking for those whose hearts are perfect toward him that he might *show his great power in helping them!*

The *power* of God that fashioned a cosmos out of chaos! The *power* of God that keeps the planets spinning in their orbits around the sun! The *power* of God that causes the seasons to roll endlessly on in perfect precision! The very *power* of God that brought Jesus Christ forth from the grave victorious over sin and death! God wants to show forth *that power in your life!* He wants to use that power to help you! What a promise!

That is not an empty promise. For this Bible is the record of the mighty workings of God's power in the lives of men from the beginning of history! Christian experience confirms that God is still keeping this promise, today. So Dave Michael said, "I believe this! I stake my life on it! I commit myself to God and he helps me!"

I was having dinner with Mr. McCormick from Birmingham, Alabama, as he told what Christ had done for him. "Before World War II, I was in the clothing business." With a twinkle in his eye, he continued, "When I went into the army, the military with its usual efficiency, put me, a clothing salesman, to driving a truck. But God used even that unhappy experience of truck driving to prepare me for what lay ahead.

"When I returned from the army, I bought an old bulldozer and started in the earth-moving business. I made a covenant to take God as my 50-50 partner and to give him, not just one tenth, but 50 percent of what we earned. My friends, and even my wife, thought I was crazy! The first year I made $3,000—and God got his 50 percent of it! The next year I made $30,000!"

Then he unfolded to me the most exciting story of how God blessed him in so many unexpected ways. He expanded into other enterprises and had recently completed a project on which the long-term profit would run into the multiple millions. He had no children of his own, but he had educated more than 45 young people for Christian and missionary work. He was now on his second generation of young people, the children of some of the first ones he had sent to college and to seminary.

Excitedly, he said, "It works! If you commit yourself wholly to God—if you commit your business to him, if you are a faithful steward, if you give God first claim on your time, your talents, and your ability—God is going to help you! I'm not saying your cow will give more milk, or that your car will get more miles per gallon of gas. But God will bless you in ways that you never dreamed, even as he has blessed me! God is looking for people he can trust so he can bless them!"

There are some young couples who are starting out in life who ought to say, "Let us make a covenant with God. We will let God rule and reign in our home, in our family affairs, in our business and financial life." God is looking for some young couples who will respond to him. He wants to show his power in your life and help you to live victorious and triumphant!

There are nominal church members, not involved in the work and witness of the church, not totally dedicated to Christ in all the affairs of your life. God wants to help you, too! Take the responsibility of a Sunday School class! Start tithing, visiting, witnessing! He wants you, in full surrender, to belong to him; and he wants to show his power by helping you!

More than a half-century ago, two sportsmen were sailing along the coast of Scotland. They anchored their yacht in the harbor at Inverness, and went ashore to roam the beautiful countryside. They became lost and could not find their way back to the harbor. At nightfall they knocked on the door of a peasant cottage and asked for a meal and lodging for the night. The farmer viewed them with suspicion and sent them away. Later they knocked at the door of a neighboring farmer. He opened wide the door and welcomed the strangers into his home. He set them before a table laden with food. He gave them bed and breakfast. Only in the morning did the farmer discover that one of the two yachtsmen was the Prince of Wales who later became Edward V, the beloved king of England.

Imagine the shame and disappointment of the first man who closed his door against his king! Imagine the joy and delight of the second man who opened his door to a stranger—and discovered that he had received his king into his house!

Today, it is no stranger that knocks at your heart. It is the King and Lord of all life, Jesus Christ. He is knocking and pleading, "Let me come in. I want to abide in your heart. I want to release in you my power, the power of Almighty God himself. I want the world to see the power of God working in your life as I help you be victorious and triumphant over all things!"

Your King has found you! Your King is here! Your King is knocking! Your King is waiting for you to respond. Will you open the door?

VIII

When the Going Gets Tough!

Luke 11:5-13; 18:1-8

"Men ought always to pray, and not to faint."

The Roman army is marching in full gear across a hot desert waste. One soldier, exhausted, faints and falls to the side! The army plunges into battle. The fighting is fierce and the going gets tough. Another soldier, weary of the conflict, throws down his weapons, sheds his armor and quits the battlefield!

This is the figure of speech Jesus applies to the battle of life. Every day is a battle! The struggle is intense. The enemy almost overcomes us. We become weary when the going is tough. Some faint and others quit!

But, Jesus says, "Men ought not to faint! Men ought not to quit!" But what shall we do when the battle of life gets tough? Grit our teeth in fresh determination? Stand and slug it out with supreme self-confidence saying, "I *can* win the battle!"

Jesus spoke a parable unto them that men ought *always to* pray! The more intense the battle, pray! The harder the task, pray! The more exhausted you are, pray! Don't faint! Don't quit! Men ought *always* to pray!

Jesus the Example

Jesus practiced what he taught. The more weary and exhausted, the more Jesus prayed! The heavier the burden, the greater the antagonism, the more massive the hostilities, the more he prayed!

Luke 11 tells of Jesus and the apostles withdrawing to a mountain retreat. The disciples were weary and anxious for sleep. But

Jesus went aside to pray. The disciples followed him and came upon the Lord kneeling in the path. They listened as he prayed. They saw his face. They saw the burden lifted as our Lord prayed to the Father. When Jesus finished, they said, "Lord, teach us to pray . . . like that!"

Many times they heard Jesus preach. But we have no account of their asking him, "Lord, teach us to *preach!*" Thousands followed to hear him teach. But we have no record of the disciples saying, "Lord, teach us to *teach!*" They witnessed his miracle-working power. But they did not ask, "Lord, teach us to do *miracles* like you!" But having seen him pray, their one overwhelming impression was his power in prayer! Jesus seemed to possess some secret, some key that unlocked the mysterious power of prayer. They had seen many other men pray—devout men praying on street corners—priests praying in the Temple. They themselves had prayed many times. But there was something about the way Jesus prayed—maybe the sincerity, the supernaturalness, the apparent power, the obvious results that caused them to say, "Lord, teach us to *pray.*" Jesus responded with a parable to illustrate how men ought to pray.

The Farmer an Example

The scene is a Palestinian home, quite different from our houses today. However, in parts of the Middle East and Europe I have seen similar housing. The house and the barn are combined. The front two thirds of the house has a hard-packed clay floor where livestock are stabled at night. At the edge of this area is a manger containing hay for the livestock. Beyond the stable area is a raised wooden platform where the family lives. Up on the living platform is the charcoal brazier where the family cooks, the sleeping mats, the baby's cradle, other personal belongings. In the cold of winter, the livestock are brought inside the house not only to protect them from robbers and wild beasts but also that their body heat might help to warm the dwelling.

Some scholars think that Jesus may have been born in such a house. The Scriptures do not say that Jesus was born in a *stable,* only that he was laid in a *manger.* There was no room for Joseph and Mary in the inn where travelers usually stayed. Perhaps they found lodging in a dwelling house, maybe with a relative or friend. But they were placed in the stable area with animals because there was no room in the tiny living quarters on the platform above and beyond the stable area. Possibly Mary and Joseph lay down on the straw with the donkey, the sheep, the cow all resting nearby. When Jesus was born, he could have been laid up above them in the safety of the manger. Be that as it may, this is the setting for the parable, a Palestinian home of Jesus' day.

The time and occasion is midnight on a bitter cold night. The farmer and his family have long since been in bed. They had no electric lights. Fuel was expensive, so it was the custom to retire at dark. The animals were bedded down. The heavy oak door closed and barred.

The family had been asleep for many hours when a neighbor knocks on the door. In a coarse whisper, the farmer calls out, "Who is it?" The answer, "Your neighbor. I'm in trouble! Guests have come to my house and I have nothing to feed them. Lend me three loaves of bread

The farmer replies, "We are all in bed. The door is shut. Go away quietly lest you wake the baby." The truth of the matter is that the farmer did not *want* to get up! It was pitch dark. The fire had gone out. The room was cold. He would have to stumble through the dark, shivering in his nightshirt, barking his shins on the furniture to get down into the stable area. Then he would have to feel his way around the sleeping animals to reach the door. He simply did not want to be bothered!

But, with a twinkle in his eye, Jesus continues the story. The neighbor keeps knocking and calling, "Open up. Loan me three loaves of bread!" The farmer pleads, "Go away and quit bothering us!" Finally, the exasperated farmer gets up, comes to the door, and gives the neighbor bread! Why? Jesus said, "Not because he was a *friend*—but because the fellow made a nuisance of himself!" And the only way to get rid of him was to grant his request. The farmer said, "I give up! Here is bread. Now begone and leave us alone."

This is the parable Jesus told about prayer. Immediately you ask, Is God like that? Is God irritated by our prayers? Are we to harass God until he answers? Does he answer our prayers only to get rid of us?" Certainly nothing could be further from the truth. Then why did Jesus tell this story? What is the point of the parable?

In some parables, Jesus said that the kingdom of heaven is *like unto*—and he draws a parallel. But not so here. He does not say that prayer or God is *like unto* the farmer in this story. Here is another kind of parallelism, not to demonstrate *similarity* but *contrast*. The key is in verse 13: "How much more. . . ." If a farmer will do this for a persistent neighbor to get rid of him because he is a nuisance, *how much more so* will a loving heavenly Father grant the request of his own children. In other words, if you or I, as a human being with a bad motive will give what is asked of us just to be rid of a bothersome visitor, how *much more so* will God, who loves us with a good motive and for a good reason give us what we ask of him as his children!

The Judge an Example

Then Jesus tells another story to make the same point, recorded in Luke 18:1-8. There was a certain judge, wicked, mean, dishonest, notorious for his crookedness. This judge responded only to bribery, or influence, or power. Everyone knew this!

There was a certain little nameless widow seeking justice from the judge. She had no money to bribe him. She had no influence or power to force him. What did she do? She just pestered him all the time begging, "Judge, give me justice!" When he came down in the morning to open court, she was waiting outside calling,

"Judge, give me justice!" In the middle of a case, she would stand up in open court and cry out, "Judge, give me justice!" When he went out for lunch with business associates, she followed him all the way into the restaurant pleading, "Judge, give me justice!" When he went home in the evening, she was waiting in front of his gate calling out, "Judge, give me justice."

The widow became such a nuisance that the judge's friends began to tease him about his "lady friend." He became so embarrassed and so harassed that this crooked unjust judge finally stopped and said, "Woman, what is it you want? Tell me and I will do it just to get rid of you!"

Jesus' conclusion is—*if* a crooked, dishonest judge, with a bad motive, will give this unknown insignificant strange widow what she asks—*how much more* so will your heavenly Father, who loves you with a pure and worthy motive, give to you, his child, what you ask!

So Jesus is saying that when the going gets tough, pray! Come to God knowing that he loves you. He cares for you. He will respond to you. If your son asks of you bread, would you give him a stone? If your son asks for a fish, would you give him a serpent? If your son asks for an egg, would you give him a scorpion? If you, as an earthly parent, know how to give good gifts to your children, *how much more* so does your heavenly Father know how to give good gifts to you. So men ought always to pray and not faint.

When You Pray

Three simple truths about prayer emerge from these two stories.

Why Pray?

1. We ought pray *because of our need.* We should not be ashamed or embarrassed to come to God and say, "Here is my desire, my wish, my need." Sometimes this is difficult because of pride. We are reluctant to acknowledge our weakness or our

need to God. But the neighbor needed bread. The woman wanted justice. Neither was embarrassed to ask for what he wanted. True prayer is not a recitation of proper words and pleasing phrases. True prayer is an open, honest, needy, childlike heart coming to a loving Father and asking for help.

So, whatever your need, ask God for it! Don't hesitate to talk to God about your examination at school, or to ask God to help you in your work, or to ask God to help and guide you in your love affairs. Just pray, "Lord, this is what I *want!* These are my *problems!* This is what I *think I need.* This may be selfish. But this is the way I feel. I also know you love me, Lord. In your love you will give me that which I need and that which is best for me!"

2. God as a loving father *waits* for you to come to him, and *wants to respond* to your request. I believe God finds joy in giving you what you ask!

I talked with a young man who was in a heap of trouble. He said, "I cannot go to my father and mother and ask them to help me. I have disobeyed and disappointed them so many times. I have already cost them so much money. I just cannot ask them to forgive me and help me again!" But I knew his parents. They loved him. I knew they were waiting and longing for their boy to come home that they might help. They wanted to share his burden. They wanted to stand by him. They wanted to give their last penny to help him. But, I am sorry to say, they could not because he would not ask them.

Never say, "I cannot ask God to help me. I have failed him. I have disobeyed him. I have rejected him. I have refused him." We cannot sin beyond the grace of God's forgiveness! We cannot stray beyond the love of God! The only barrier between his love and your sin is *your own will.*

We should pray because we have needs. And the greater the need the more we should pray! So Jesus said, "Men ought always to pray."

How to Pray

1. Jesus gave no instructions about the *physical posture* for prayer. Some may kneel. Others may pray standing with bowed heads. In Jesus' day, some prayed looking up to God with arms outstretched. I do not consider the position of the body important; but the stance of the heart is very important!

2. In these two stories, Jesus tells us that we are to *go directly* to God. The advertisement of the telephone company says, "Don't write—talk by long distance to your loved one person-to-person." When my children were in college, they took this advertisement seriously! We expected a weekly letter from them. But on Saturday night, the phone would ring. The operator would ask, "Will you accept the charges for a collect call?" It would be one of the children explaining, "I have been so busy this week. I haven't had time to write. I just wanted to talk to you and tell you I'm all right." Of course, I fussed about the telephone bill. But deep inside I was really quite glad to pay it. It is so good to talk person-to-person with someone you love! So it is with God!

Recently I was visiting a church member in the hospital. In an adjoining bed was a woman of another faith. Discovering that I was a minister, she handed me her prayer book and requested that I read a prayer for her. I said, "These prayers are beautifully expressed, but let me just close the prayer book and pray our own prayer directly to God. What is it that you would like for me to tell God about yourself, and ask him to do for you?" And the dear woman asked, "Can you do that?" Somehow she had been led to believe that she was not capable of making up her own prayers. She had to read or recite prayers that her church had prepared for her.

So I prayed for her and then suggested, "Now, why don't you pray by just talking to God as you have talked to me, telling him what is in your heart?" She prayed and wept in joy with the realization that for the first time in her life she had gone *directly* to God, *person-to-person*, in prayer.

3. Then we are to be *frank and honest* with God. Tell God what is in your heart.

Some years ago I called on a man who had visited in our church services. As we talked, I learned that he was from the mountains, had murdered a man in a family feud, and had a prison record. He knew little about religion. But he had a deep sense of guilt and wanted to be forgiven and saved by God. After reading Romans 3:23, I explained how all men are lost because all have sinned . . . all must confess their sins to God and truly repent . . . I explained how Christ had died for our sins . . . and if we will receive him into our heart as Lord and Savior, he will forgive us and save us.

With quivering lips he stammered, "But I have been such a wicked man. Do you think he would forgive me?" I said, "Why don't you ask him and see?" "But how can I ask him?" I said, "Pray to him." With a sign of hopelessness he said, "That's the trouble, I don't know how to pray." I asked him, "Would you like for me to teach you to pray?" He nodded, and so we knelt together. I instructed him, "Now, just talk to God, like you have been talking to me. Tell him all about yourself, about how you feel and what you want him to do for you."

So, with faltering words he began. He did not use a single theological word. He knew nothing about the doctrine of justification, atonement, or repentance. But frankly, and honestly, he told God he was sorry; he wanted Christ to forgive him; he wanted to live for Jesus in a new life. And when we were through, he stood on his feet a converted man with tears of joy streaming down his face. I still hear from him occasionally. He has served the Lord faithfully through the years and is now teaching a Sunday School class.

4. So, when you pray, go directly—be frank—and *be persistent!* Remember the neighbor kept knocking on the farmer's door! The woman kept harassing the judge!

Does this mean that if we keep harassing God, he will finally give in and grant us our requests? I don't think so. But I do know that *persistent prayer* is to *help us*. Persistence helps refine our prayers. Many things we request are often passing fancies. We ask today, but by tomorrow we have forgotten our request. But when we pray persistently and consistently, that prayer may become a consuming passion that refines our goals and our purposes.

So John Knox prayed, "Oh, God, give me Scotland or I die." He did not pray this prayer only one time, or for only one day, or for only one week, or one month, or one year! He prayed this prayer, day on day without end, into the years. Just because John Knox was persistent in prayer, God did not gather up all the Scottish people and deliver them in a package to John Knox saying, "You asked for them—here they are, John Knox." No! But God *did* give John Knox Scotland! Knox's persistent prayer solidified his goals, focused his purposes, refined his desires, until he was possessed by one all-consuming passion. And he poured out his life to that end.

Rewards of Prayer

The *result* of prayer is this: God always responds!

1. God always gives us our *needs,* but not always our *askings.* Frequently, what we ask for is *not* what we need. At other times we are not even aware of our needs to ask for them! But when we pray, God always responds to provide our needs.

Remember, the farmer in the story gave his neighbor the *bread that he needed!* The neighbor only asked for three loaves. But he probably needed a *dozen.* For they were small flat cake-like loaves hardly larger than biscuits. The farmer said, "Here, take what you need!"

So we come to God not fully aware of our need, but God always supplies it. Paul asked three times that his thorn in the flesh be removed. But instead of granting his request, God gave Paul what he really needed, courage, strength, and endurance to overcome his burden. He gave Paul a witness through his suffering. So with us, God gives his grace, his forgiveness, his strength, all of that which we need to face life.

2. Above all, when we pray, God gives himself to us. A child comes asking an earthly father for something unreasonable and impossible. What does the human parent do? He responds saying, "No, daddy cannot give you what you ask." Then reaching out, he gathers the child in his arms and says, "But daddy loves you and will give you something so much better. One day you will understand."

So, when we pray, God always gives himself to us. We feel his presence. We receive his power. We recieve him. So, when the going gets tough, let us faint not, but always pray. Even right now, let us pray!

IX

Short Beds and Narrow Covers

Isaiah 28:18-20

The text quickens a nostalgic memory of childhood days for many of us. We recall a Christmas visit to the farm to see Grandmother. It is a blustery winter night. Snow is on the ground. We are sent to a cold unheated second-story bedroom to sleep. The wind rattles the shutters and whistles through the windows. And your bed is too short, the covers too narrow, and you shiver through a sleepless night.

This is a homey proverb spoken by Isaiah to the intelligentsia of Jerusalem. The nation was at peace with their neighbors. It was a time of great prosperity and affluence. The people were living in luxury, literally on "beds of ease." They never had it so good! Yet, in spite of their ivory couches, Isaiah said, "Your bed is too short and your cover too narrow!" The prophet used this figure of speech to say that their religion was inadequate!

Strike the parallel today! We too recline on beds of ease and affluence. We never had it so good! Modern technology has given us comfort and convenience beyond the wildest dreams of our forefathers. Popular religion is booming. Churches are full! Our historical faith has a nominal acceptance in the structures of our culture. But deep inside us there is the gnawing suspicion that it is all quite superficial. Spiritually, our bed is too short and the cover too narrow!

Examine your faith. What does your religion *really* mean to you? What does it give you? Do you possess all that God wants to give you and do for you? In other words, "How adequate is your religion?"

A Conscious Knowledge of Sin Forgiven

Your religion is inadequate if it has not given you a conscious knowledge of sin forgiven. If you do not live daily with a cleansed feeling inside, knowing that the burden of guilt has been lifted, and you have been delivered from the judgment and power of sin, then your faith is inadequate! If you cannot walk with head up and spirit high boldly declaring that "God through Jesus Christ has forgiven me," you have less than God has promised or desires for you!

Many years ago I baptized a man who had been a member of the notorious Al Capone crime syndicate. He had served time in Leavenworth. He told me that he had been converted while in prison. He had only a smattering of Bible knowledge and little understanding of the Christian life when I first met him. But I had no doubt about the genuineness of his conversion.

I asked, "Paul, you say you confessed your sins and gave your heart to Jesus in prison. How do you know that Jesus has saved you?" With a twinkle in his eye he fired back, "I know! Because my pillow isn't hard anymore." Smiling he continued, "After I gave my heart to Jesus, I could sleep at night without that overwhelming sense of guilt, that terrible self-condemnation, that depressing despair inside me. It was all lifted and I felt all clean inside. Ever since then I sleep at night—on a soft pillow!"

That is exactly what God has promised for each of us! If your pillow is hard, then yours is a short bed and a narrow cover, spiritually!

A deeply distressed married woman came to my study and said, "I have committed the unpardonable sin!" She had become involved in a love triangle and in tears poured out a confession of adultery and infidelity. In spite of my assurances that adultery was not the unpardonable sin, she continued to say, "God will never forgive me."

Then I simply asked, "Do you believe the Bible is true?" "Do you believe God is honest and will do what he promises?" She answered, "Yes, of course." Then I read, "If we confess our sins, he is faithful and just to forgive us our sins, and to cleanse us from *all* unrighteousness" (1 John 1:9). Then I asked, "Does it say *some* unrighteousness? Or all unrighteousness *except* adultery? Or does *all* include what you have done?" She said, "I guess it means *all* sin." I asked, "Now what does God ask you to do? *You confess*—and *he forgives*."

As we knelt together she confessed her sins to God, and asked forgiveness through Jesus Christ, and committed her life to him as Lord. And because she did in faith what God commanded, he did by grace what he had promised. And she stood with tears of joy streaming down her face with the assurance of God's forgiveness and acceptance in her heart!

You may belong to a dozen churches, be baptized in every form and manner practiced in Christendom, and have a knowledge of the Bible from cover to cover—but if you do not have a conscious knowledge of sin forgiven, and certainty that your sins have been removed as far as the east is from the west—you have not received the full joy and peace that God wants to give you through Jesus Christ.

The Assurance of Salvation

There is a second short bed and narrow cover. Your faith is inadequate if it does not give you the *assurance* of salvation. Eternal life is to be a present-tense possession, not merely a future hope!

Salvation is both a *status* and a *process*. The believer's *relationship* as a son of God is established when we are born again. A son born into the family is always the child and heir of his parents. And the believer born into God's family is from the beginning and forevermore God's child and heir.

Yet we are continually possessing our sonship day by day. So, in one sense, the Christian is saved the moment he believes and has "everlasting life, and shall not come into condemnation; but is passed from death unto life" as Jesus promised (John 5:24). But, in another sense, the Christian is being saved day by day and will be saved at the last day. So Paul speaks of our "hope of salvation" (1 Thess. 5:8) and "hope of eternal life" (Titus 3:7) and 1 Peter 1:5 speaks of the believer "kept by the power of God through faith unto salvation ready to be revealed in the last time."

So our salvation is something already possessed, yet it is also something to be fulfilled or received at a future date. You ask, "How can that be—something yet to be *received*—yet at the same time *already possessed?*" There is no contradiction. Consider this analogy. The proud father says, "I already have a savings program for my newborn son's education. I am buying bonds in his name." So the father has said to his son, "I am giving you these bonds, *now*. They are *now* in your name. Legally they are already your possession. But their full benefits and blessings will not be yours until later when you go to college. They are yours first in the beginning—but they are also yours yet to be claimed in the future!"

So God, through Jesus Christ's death on the cross has purchased eternal life for the believer. When we receive him as Savior in personal commitment and faith, salvation becomes our present-tense possession. While there are future blessings and benefits yet to be claimed, we have the *title deed*, the *Assurance of possession*, right now!

God does not want you to be suspended in a constant state of anxiety about your salvation. You are not to live with an uncertain hope that you *will* be saved, hopefully striving for eternal life. The Bible says, "These things have I written unto you that believe on the name of the Son of God; that ye may *know that ye have eternal life . . .* " (1 John 5:13).

Again, the Holy Spirit confirms the assurance of our salvation. Upon hearing and believing the gospel we are "sealed with that holy Spirit" dwelling within us. The Holy Spirit is God's promise or pledge that our redemption will be completed. He speaks again and again of the *earnest* of the Spirit (Eph. 1:14, etc.). That Greek word means literally "pledge money" that a person puts up as a forfeit to guarantee that he will not go back on a contract or an agreement, but will carry out his part of the contract. The Holy Spirit is God's guarantee that we shall enter into the full possession of our inheritance of salvation and eternal life.

Jesus himself gave us the assurance of salvation and eternal life as a present-tense irrevocable possession of the believer. Jesus called himself "the good shepherd," and you and me as believers, "his sheep." He said, "*My* sheep hear *my* voice and I know them, and they follow me" (John 10:27). Those of us who have followed him, belong to him! We are *his* and he is *ours!* Then he continues, "I *give* unto them *eternal* life . . . . " He does say, "I *will* give" in some distant future—but right now "I give." He does not say merely abundant life, enrichment of life, a joy-filled life, but *eternal* life. You may stray, slip and fall into sin, but you cannot fall away from this *eternal* life that Christ has given you.

Sin and death cannot terminate that life. For by the very definition of the word "eternal," if that life could be terminated by any failure on your part, activity on the devil's part, or change of mind on God's part, it could not be called *eternal.* For that life to be *tentative* and *contingent* would be a contradiction of the essential meaning of the word "eternal." So Jesus promised "Unto *my* sheep who *follow me,* I now give them *eternal* life."

Then, as Jesus had done many times as a boy in Joseph's carpenter shop, driving home a nail in a piece of furniture with repeated solid blows of the hammer, Jesus drives home this glorious truth of the assurance of eternal life by saying the same thing in another way. "And they shall *never* perish" (v. 28).

Then again, as in the carpenter shop, he had often turned over the board and clenched the nail, Jesus wanted to make sure that no one would ever misunderstand his promise of absolute security for the believer. He clenches this promise of assurance by saying,

"Neither shall any man pluck them out of my hand" (v. 28). Our security rests not upon our own strength to hold onto Jesus Christ, to walk daily free from sin, to follow faithfully in his service—but upon the power of Jesus Christ to hold onto us! And Jesus said that in his hand is the very *power of God* himself, "My Father, which gave them me, is greater than all; and no man is able to pluck them out of my *Father's hand*" (v. 29).

God wants to give you today the confident assurance of salvation and eternal life. Anxiety, doubt, uncertainty, anything less than the joy and security of full assurance is a short bed and a narrow cover.

Compassion and Concern for Human Need

There is another short bed and narrow cover. Your faith is inadequate if it fails to produce compassion and concern for human need. Again and again we read that Jesus "looked with compassion upon the multitudes." When we become a child of God, we should begin to see the world through the eyes of Jesus. We see people needing love, care, help, both physical and spiritual. We see people to whom we must minister in the name of Christ regardless of the color of skin, or cut of clothes, or social status.

Today, we hear a great deal about the conflict between social action and evangelism. A new humanism emphasizes social action. Because man is the supreme value in life, we must minister to people simply because they are people! We are to minister to physical need because there is physical need! Social ministry is to be an end in itself, for man's sake!

But this new humanism has encountered a problem, it has been unable to motivate people to selfless social service. It has said, "You *ought* to do good to your fellowman." But men do not *do* good—because they *are* not good, inside. The problem is man himself. It just does not work to merely *ask* man to treat his human brother in a brotherly way! Something must happen first to change the selfish, egocentric nature of man before he is stirred to compassionate selfless service to others.

We cannot have meaningful social action without evangelism first. The unregenerate human heart must first be transformed by the power of God. The nature of God must be revived in man and he must be fashioned anew in the likeness of Christ to see the world through God's eyes and love men as Christ loved them! Social action without evangelism is a short bed and a narrow cover!

Evangelism is the primary task of the church. Evangelism is a priority task. It is evangelism that must first undergird the social action of the state. So let the church concentrate on its unique ministry of evangelism in order that it might produce an enlightened state that can then effectively deal with the great issues of poverty, war, racial prejudice, ecological crisis, etc.

But on the other hand, too many times we have seen a sterile evangelism that was simply concerned with saving the *souls* of men and showed little compassion for the *whole* man and no concern for the unjust structure of the society in which he lived. Evangelism that is not concerned about injustice, social inequities, poverty, prejudice, is also a short bed and a narrow cover!

However, I cannot accept the blanket indictment of the social activists who have ridiculed all evangelism and condemned the established evangelical churches. Through the centuries, when no other social or political structure cared about human need, evangelical churches have been building schools and colleges, hospitals, and orphanages. Devout Christians have given their time, energy, and monies for these causes at home and through mission enterprises around the world. We as evangelicals have a great tradition in social action and let no one deny it!

And let no one fault this local church! We at Walnut Street, like many others, are evangelistic to the core. But we have a great Christian social ministry. We have our clothing shop, food closet, the high-rise apartment for the elderly, our mental health clinic, the youth drug rehabilitation house, the tutoring program, the vast weekday Christian activities and recreation program—these and many other ministries done in the name of Christ to all people regardless of race or status! And these things we do because of our commitment to a basic philosophy: *The whole gospel—for the whole man—to the whole of humanity—in the whole world.*

Personal Integrity

There is yet another short bed and narrow cover. Your faith is inadequate if it does not produce personal integrity. Whether a student, an office worker, a businessman, a housewife, a boy or girl, man or woman—when you become a Christian, it should give you a new set of moral ideals that produces personal integrity.

I was preaching in the interior of Guatemala in the little Indian village, San Pedro, on the shores of Lake Antigua. I met many wonderful converted Indians. The missionary interpreted the testimony of one named George for me, "Yes, when I became a believer, it made me see my duty!" I asked George what he meant and he replied, "Well, when I became a Christian, it made me see my duty to my children. When I was unconverted, they often went hungry. It made me see my duty to my wife. When I was a sinner, I was often unfaithful. It made me see my duty on my job. I was a thief, a liar, and lazy. But now I am honest, and work hard. It made me pay my debts. It made me quit drinking. It made me see my duty!"

How simple, and yet how profound! That is exactly what is supposed to happen when you and I become a Christian. It should make us "see our duty." Remember when Zacchaeus met Jesus at Jericho. The little tax gatherer had been unjust and unfair but when he was converted he said, "I have been unethical in my business dealings, and I want to make restitution fourfold because I have met Jesus Christ." If your Christian experience has not given you integrity, honesty; made you a better person, a better worker, a better mate, a better child; given you a deeper feeling of moral responsibility to others and to society; made you say, "I see my duty"—then it is a short bed and a narrow cover!

Love for the Church

There is another short bed. Your faith is inadequate if it does not produce loyalty, love, devotion, and service in the church of Jesus Christ. I read in the book of Acts that those who believed "were baptized and added to the church!" I do not say that you cannot be a Christian without being a member of the church. You may be saved any time, any place that you accept Jesus Christ as your Savior. But you cannot be an adequate full-grown fruit-bearing Christian outside the church.

It is only natural and normal that if you are a child of God, you will love the other members of God's family and want to be with them. So 1 John 3:14 says, "We know that we have passed from death unto life, because we love the brethren."

Hope for Tomorrow

Finally, a last short bed and narrow cover! Your faith is inadequate if it does not give you a sense of security about the future, a hope and joyful expectation for tomorrow. As a Christian, we can put our loved ones into God's care without distress or anxiety or great sorrow, to pass through death and the grave into the presence of God! As a Christian, we can trust our own tomorrows to God. We can truly sing, "I know not what the future holds, but I know who holds the future!"

Dr. Carter Helm Jones, an eloquent pulpiteer of another generation, told of his grandfather moving from Charleston after the Civil War. He had lost his wife and his property in the war. He was left alone with only an old Negro servant, a former slave. The Negro and the old man loaded their few belongings in a wagon hitched to a team of mules and started on a long journey to another community to begin a new life.

They began after dark with the Negro driving and the old man, exhausted and discouraged, stretched out in the bed of the wagon to sleep. Sometime during the night he was awakened. The mules had stopped and the driver was gone from the seat. Then he heard a groaning beside the wagon. He sat up and saw the old Negro kneeling on the ground, praying and crying, "Oh, Master Jones, it is the end of the world! Pray to God; ask him to save us!" Then looking up he saw they were in the midst of a meteorite shower. Falling stars were zooming all around them in the sky. He spoke softly to the old Negro, "It is not the end of the world. Get back on the wagon and drive the mules on down the road. Do you see that star?" he asked pointing to the North Star. "Just keep your eye on that star. If it falls, wake me up. But as long as that star is in the sky, you can know that it is not the end of the world and everything is all right."

God has put some stars in the sky for us as Christians—the star of his love, of his grace, of his forgiveness, of his assurance of eternal life in him, of prayer by which we can make our petitions known to him. Until these stars fall, we need not worry or be anxious. And they will not fall!

When you begin to feel that it is the end of the world for you, look up and see these stars in the sky and know that this world and your life are still in God's hands, and all is well! This is the kind of faith, and peace, and assurance God wants to give you today through Jesus Christ!

X

The Backhand of God

Romans 1:18-32 (TLB)

The time is July 8, 1741. The setting, a church in Enfield, Massachusetts. In the pulpit is a frail man with weak eyesight holding a full sermon manuscript. He begins reading in a deliberate and methodical manner to a passive audience. Before the service is over, however, throughout the congregation there is shouting and weeping, quivering and fainting! People are holding to the back of pews or clinging to pillars to keep from falling into hell. A fellow preacher tugs at the coattails of the pastor, attempting to pull him down and pleading, "Mr. Edwards, Mr. Edwards, is not God also merciful?"

The preacher was Jonathan Edwards. His sermon was "Sinners in the Hands of an Angry God." His sermon had dealt with the wrath and judgment of God. Dramatically he pictured God as the archer with drawn bow and the arrow aimed at the sinner's heart. He described the sinner an an ugly gruesome spider hanging by a single thread over the flames of hell. When the service was done, one of the greatest revivals of Colonial America had broken out.

The Preaching of Judgment

You say that such preaching would certainly not get a hearing *today!* Hellfire-and-brimstone preaching is not popular! But it was not popular then!

But, you say, this must have been a very *ignorant congregation* and an *unlettered preacher*. Hardly so. For the man in the pulpit has been adjudged as one of the most brilliant men of American history and appraised by some as the greatest mind in Colonial America. A renowned scholar and theologian, a man of culture, training, talents, and ability, he later became president of Princeton University. Likewise the congregation was equally cultured and sophisticated.

The response of the congregation can be explained only in terms of the universal truth and awesome reality of the theme of the sermon. Jonathan Edwards was preaching on the *inescapable inevitable judgment of God upon sinful men*. This theme is a lost chord in much of our preaching today. Nevertheless, judgment is a central theme of the Bible, a reality of history, and a certainty of eternity!

We do well to talk about the eternal and matchless love of God. For the essential nature of God is love! We do well to picture that love as an outstretched pleading hand extended to all men. But, as my hand has one side, a palm which is distinctive—my hand has yet another side when turned over—a backhand, totally different from the palm. So the outstretched hand of God's love has an opposite side—the backhand of God is the judgment of God! God's judgment upon sin is as much a part of his essential nature as God's love for the sinner.

So Paul wrote in Romans 1:18, "God *shows* his *anger* from heaven against all sinful, evil men." That is the backhand of God! The King James translation says, "the *wrath* of God is *revealed* against all *ungodliness* and *unrighteousness.*"

So God shows his anger from heaven against the ungodliness and unrighteousness of men. *Ungodliness* is a *vertical* relationship. It is a sin of attitude, of irreligion, resulting in alienation from God. *Unrighteousness* is *horizontal*, wrongdoing toward other men, resulting in alienation from man. Ungodliness and unrighteousness are interrelated, the first produces the second. Alienation from God results in alienation from our fellowman.

The Sin of Ungodliness

Paul gives examples of our ungodliness.

Idolatry

In verse 23 he says that ungodly men have changed the glory of God into an image, or an *idol.* Instead of worshiping the living God, men worship idols of "wood and stone and of themselves." Instead of worshiping the God who made all things, men have worshiped the things God made.

If a visitor from outer space were to drop in on our culture and observe that earth creatures worshiped idols, we would be greatly offended. We would say, "How ridiculous. We believe in God. We are very religious. See our churches! Our many expressions of religion!" But Paul says that it is the object of our worship, the object of our faith, the object of our commitment—not our theological affirmations or our forms of worship—that determine whether we are idolators. *Idolatry is to worship that which is created instead of the creator himself!*

1. For example, there is the idol of *scientism.* Heady with the wine of space conquest, we have come to believe that man is on the threshold of his greatest era of advancement. Deep in our hearts many of us believe that science is now capable of delivering man from his every problem. Given time, our computerized applied science will ultimately bring us to a utopia. *In* ourselves, and *of* ourselves *we will* resolve our ecological crises, our energy crisis, our economic crisis, our political crisis. The capacity of the human mind is unlimited! The human spirit is unconquerable!

Several years ago on a visit to Russia, I picked up a propaganda pamphlet in the Moscow Airport. It was written in English for tourists. Published by the Novasti press agency, it was entitled, *What Is Communism, Questions and Answers.* Portions of it read as follows; "As proponents of a materialistic philosophy, we accept only a scientific and not a religious explanation of all the things and phenomena we encounter in nature and society . . . we reject religion for the simple reason that we have faith in the omnipotence of the human intellect and believe in the natural origin of everything on earth . . . . The Soviet state and Communist Party are instilling in people the belief in scientific, atheistic ideology. . . . We are sure that the religious conceptions of life, nature, man and his place, role, destination, just as all other superstitions and prejudices, will gradually disappear altogether in the process of building a new society. . . . Every member of a communist society will have faith only in his own energy, his work, in the unlimited creative potentiality of his free spirit, in his bright mind, equipped with the all-conquering force of knowledge."

We are appalled at such open avowed theoretical atheism. But we are *practical atheists*—idolaters, Paul would say because we have put our trust in scientific technology to deliver us. We are worshiping the creature and the created instead of the creator.

2. Then there is the idol of *materialism*. An idol is that which claims your first interest, your ultimate loyalty, your heart's devotion. Paul says, "You say, 'Don't pray to idols' and then make money your God instead" (v. 22). So we are idolators saying "holy, holy *dollar;* holy, holy *business;* holy, holy beautiful well-kept suburban *home;* holy, holy weekend lake *cottage!*" Whatever is absorbing the interest of your life, that is your god! Idolatry is giving ourselves to the created *thing* instead of the *creator* himself!

3. There is the idol of *humanism*. A basic flaw in human nature is an irresistible "god almightiness" within us. Satan appealed to this god-ego in Adam when he whispered, "Eat of the fruit and you will be equal to God."

In every man there is this unregenerate compulsion to *be God* instead of *serving God*. The Bible dramatically pictures every man standing before the judgment bar with God on the bench. And every man must give an account of himself unto God. But man wants to change the appointment and reverse the role. Man wants to sit on the bench. Man wants to put God at the judgment bar. We would have the Son of God to stand before our judgment seat subject to our whim and choice as Christ stood before Pilate. In Romans 1:22 Paul says, "Claiming themselves to be wise without God, they became utter fools instead." Wise men sit in judgment upon the word of God, the church of God, the Son of God. What fools we are to make God the Creator, subject to the judgment of the creature he has made.

4. There is the idol of *sensualism*—the insatiable drive to satisfy the animal appetite as the fulfillment of life. Paul says they are continually looking for new ways of sinning. This is the libertine "playboy" morality of our day. Sensualism is another form of idolatry, to satisfy the creature to the neglect of the creator!

Truth for a Lie

Paul says the second manifestation of ungodliness is that they have changed the truth of God into a lie (v. 25). Instead of believing the truth as given by God, they have deliberately chosen heresy, deceit, lies.

1. For example, the *Bible* is the divinely inspired record of God's mighty saving acts and dealings with the human race, climaxed by his ultimate revelation and redemptive act in Jesus Christ. Yet men deliberately reject this truth, and twist it around to believe a lie.

I sat in an interdenominational mission conference and heard a man with an air of sophisticated arrogance say, "Our people do not believe in sending missionaries into foreign cultures to *change* the people. They have a cultural religion that human expereience has proven to be valid and adequate for them. We should not try to proselyte Buddhists or Muslims to Christianity. We should not approach them with the superior attitude that we have a better religion. We should synthesize our religion with theirs and learn from them!"

This is the ungodliness that Paul condemns. It is a shameless *lie* substituted for the *truth* that Peter proclaimed before Annas the high priest and the Jews gathered in Jerusalem, "Neither is there salvation in any other: for there is none other name under heaven given among men, whereby we must be saved" (Acts 4:12).

2. Another lie that has been exchanged for truth is that it makes no difference *what* you believe—just so you do *believe* something, believe it *sincerely* and *practice* it daily! It does make a difference *what* you believe! World War II was fought over what somebody *believed!* A nation of people was led to believe in a superior Aryan race. Six million people were murdered because a people believed that the Jews were inferior human beings. There is *belief* that is hellism. There is *practice* that is godless. There is *sincerity* that is devilish. So Paul says that ungodly men have taken the *truth* of God and changed it into a lie!

Rejected Knowledge

The third manifestation of ungodliness is that men have rejected the knowledge of God already received (vv. 20-21). Men have known of God from the earliest times.

1. They have known of his existence through the very nature of his *creation*. They see the *watch* but have denied the existence of a *watchmaker*. They have seen God's handiwork but will not acknowledge his existence or worship him with their thanks.

2. Men have known God through their *conscience*. God's law has been "written within them" in men's conscience. In Romans 2:15 Paul says, "Their own conscience accuses them or sometimes excuses them." A sense of right and wrong is instinctive within man's nature. Instinctive conscience condemns wrong. Every man at all times in history had some revelation of the truth from God, but in his ungodliness he has rejected this knowledge.

The Wrath of God

Paul says, "We know God will punish anyone who does such things" (Rom. 2:2). We agree! Surely the wrath of God is upon such ungodliness! But like an arrow straight to the mark, Paul says in the next verse, "Do you think that God will judge and condemn others for doing them and overlook you when you do them, too?" You are under the same condemnation as they are! Paul was speaking to the Jews who said, "We are God's chosen people. God will excuse us."

Do we not have this same "chosen people" complex? Do we not believe that God was uniquely present in the founding of our nation established on the great Judeo-Christian ideals? Do we not salute our flag pledging "this nation *under God*"? Do we not have on our coins "In God We Trust"? Surely God will take these things into consideration and deal with us differently than the Red Communist Chinese! Or the godless Russians! Or the Muslim Arabs! Are we not in a special position of privilege—a chosen people!

Paul declares that all are under the divine wrath of God. All are guilty! None are excused!

So all men are indicted for their ungodliness and unrighteousness. The verdict is guilty! And the *anger* or *wrath* of God will be made manifest against men (1:18).

What is the *wrath* or *anger* of God? Is it an emotion? Human anger is an emotion. At 3 A.M. your fourteen-year-old son, without a driver's license, takes the keys to the family car from your dresser and slips out of the house for a joyride. He has an accident and is apprehended by the police. After you bail him out of trouble, you discipline him verbally and physically! The next day at school he tells his friends, "What a licking my father gave me! Was he angry! I really suffered the *wrath* of my father!"

So we tend to think of the wrath of God as the activity of our heavenly Father, spanking us and administering punishment and imposing penalties upon us for our disobedience. He is angry at us because of our sins. So we have imagined God hurling thunderbolts and sending earthquakes and destroying cities with volcanoes because, like an earthly father, God became angry with the disobedience of his children! But this is a mistaken and unworthy picture of the wrath of God. The wrath of God is *not* an *emotional reaction* to our wrongdoing.

The wrath of God is the *abiding inner nature of God's resistance to sin and to unrighteousness.* It is God's loving nature, his holy nature, his pure nature, so structured in the universe and in nature and in law so that it is *contrary to and automatically against all unrighteousness and sin.*

Structured in the universe is natural law. The law of gravity is an example. If I jump from the top of the church tower defying the law of gravity, I am caught up in the *wrath* of that law. It is not that God is angry with me for jumping from the tower and he breaks my leg in wrath! Disobedience of natural law produces the *wrath* of natural law!

In the same way God has structured his universe with moral law. Sin is a violation of that law. When we sin, we project our lives into the framework of God's orderly moral law and are caught up by it. His wrath comes upon us, *not because he is angry, but because we have sinned!*

Just as the love of God is like the sun, shining on the good and bad alike, so the wrath of God operates in the same universal way.

Even the wrath of the law is an expression of the *love* of God, not the *anger* of God. For God made the law of gravity so that I might live in an orderly world and know what to expect. What kind of a God would he be—what kind of love would it be—if God said, "I will allow the law of gravity to operate any way it wants to"? Suppose one day I poured a bucket of scalding water into the sink and it went down the drain. But the next day, I poured boiling water in the sink and it came *up* and scalded my face! What kind of world would this be? The very fact that the wrath of the law operates consistently to punish those who break it and to bless those who obey it as a manifestation, not of the *anger* of God, but of the love of God.

So, the fact that *judgment* comes upon us when we sin, and the *wrath* of God descends in punishment upon us, is but the *backhand* of the *loving hand* of God extended to us.

The writer of Hebrews says that it is a "fearful thing to fall into the hands of the living God" (10:31). In other words, it is an awful thing to be caught up in this process of sin and retribution. It is an awful thing to fall from a church tower and be broken on the pavement below! It is an awful thing to be caught in the power of gravity and destroyed by it! It is an awful thing to fall into the power of sin and be caught up in the consequences of retribution and be destroyed by the *wrath* of God!

The Judgment of God

Then Paul follows with a terrible judgment upon ungodliness and unrighteousness. "So God let them go" (Rom. 1:24). "When God let go of them" (v. 26), he allowed the moral law to catch them up and proceed in its operation. And they fell into the most horrible of sins.

So we have this terrible picture of a morally depraved and corrupt society . . . a godless society, without character, without charity, without conscience—sinking deeper and deeper into the cesspool of perversion—sexual deviations, homosexuality—all kinds of abuse, and dishonesty! Women turned against God's natural plan, sex sin, men burning for lust for each other, greed, hate, envy, murder, fighting, lying, bitterness, gossip, backbiting, haters of God, insolent (Rom. 1:26-31).

Is there a parallel for us today in this graphic passage? Violent crime! Lawlessness! The erosion of the moral foundations of society! Drugs and alcoholism! Sexual perversions! Homosexuality! The secularization of our society! Desecration of the Lord's Day! Broken homes! Crime on the streets! This is the wrath of God in operation. This is the end of a society of ungodly and unrighteous men—when God lets them go! A secular, sexual, violent, criminal society, going down on an escalator into self-destruction.

The Acquittal

Is there a way out? Is destruction inevitable? Are men hopelessly trapped on this descending escalator? Godless, unrighteous, sinking deeper we are unable to deliver ourselves from the judgment and wrath of God. Is there any way out?

After painting this terrible picture of this lost society, Paul makes clear the way out.

Paul says that only by God's grace can we be delivered. God has acted in the cross to provide a way out. He will acquit us and declare us "not guilty" through what Jesus Christ has done. The Bible says, "But now God has shown us a different way to heaven—not by 'being good enough' and trying to keep his laws, but by a new way. Now God says he will accept and acquit us—declare us 'not guilty'—if we trust Jesus Christ to take away our sins. And we all can be saved in this same way, by coming to Christ, no matter who we are or what we have been like. Yes, all have sinned; all fall short of God's glorious ideal; yet now God declares us 'not guilty' of offending him if we trust in Jesus Christ, who in his kindness freely takes away our sins.

"For God sent Christ Jesus to take the punishment for our sins and to end all God's anger against us. He used Christ's blood and our faith as the means of saving us from his wrath" (see Rom. 3:21-25, TLB).

Notice God has shown us a "new way of deliverance." It is not by "being good enough." Moral reformation will not deliver us. The escalator is going down. A man may run back up a few steps at a time but the escalator's direction is always down! We can never be good enough or reform enough to race to the top of the escalator and jump off!

This acquittal and deliverance is yours today through Jesus Christ. "His blood and our faith" is God's means of saving us from his wrath.

XI

Living in the Suburbs

Mark 12:28-34

Living in the suburbs is a typical American way of life. The suburbanite wants the advantages of urban culture but lives outside the city limits to escape the taxes and problems of the city.

Likewise, spiritually, there are those who live in the suburbs of the kingdom of God. They live just across the border, just outside the kingdom of God. They are just beyond the responsibilities and the commitments of the kingdom. They are spiritual suburbanites, living near to, but not in, the kingdom of God.

In our text we read of such a man. It was Tuesday, four days before Jesus was crucified. On Monday Jesus had cleared the Temple courtyard of the money changers and those who bought and sold sacrifices. Jesus' action infuriated the chief priests and the scribes. This Galilean peasant had no authority to take such violent action, neither was he a licensed teacher. But the crowds supported him. So they had determined their strategy. As the crowd of worshipers gathered, the chief priests, scribes, and elders began their questioning to "entangle him in his talk."

The Sadducees asked him a puzzling question about the resurrection. The Pharisees tried to ensnare him on the question of paying tribute to Caesar. Jesus answered so discreetly, they dared not ask him further questions. Then a lawyer, a student of the Scriptures, asked, "Which is the first commandment?"

In Judaism there were at least 600 laws that a devoutly religious person was required to obey. They were classified as weightier laws and lesser laws. The measure of righteousness, the measure of religion, the measure of faithfulness was the extent to which a person lived up to these laws. Of course, it was impossible to keep all these laws—but a person could achieve grades of righteousness as measured by the number of laws kept and the classification of the laws kept. Faced with this confusing problem of scaling righteousness, the lawyer comes right to the point, "Since it is impossible for a person to keep all 600 laws, tell me, which is the one law more important than all the rest?"

Jesus answered that the first is, "Thou shalt love the Lord thy God with all thy heart, and with all thy soul, and with all thy mind, and with all thy strength." That is, let your total person be totally committed to God.

And the second involves a similar commitment of love, "Thou shalt love thy neighbour as thyself." This vertical relationship (with God) and this horizontal relationship (with man) are to be at the center of your life. On these two laws rest all the law and the prophets. All righteousness evolves and stems from these two laws. All law is a reflection and extension of these two laws!

The lawyer looked around the Temple area and saw the many expressions of religion and the many practices of righteousness. He saw sacrifices of blood and burnt offerings of whole animals. He heard the monotonous prayers recited loud and long by the worshipers. He observed the many Temple rituals. And he said, "Right, Master. Certainly to obey these two laws is more important than all the sacrifices, all the rites, all the rituals of religion."

Perceiving that he had answered discreetly with an understanding heart, Jesus declared, "Thou art not far from the kingdom." You are living in the suburbs. You are camped right on the border, not far from the kingdom!

Some Are Far

Some are *far* from the kingdom of God.

The *hate-filled heart* is far from the kingdom. Jesus saw in the Temple crowd those who were plotting to kill him. They harbored bitterness, hatred, jealousy, and prejudice in their hearts. Even though they had gathered in the Temple to worship God, they were far from the kingdom.

It is possible to be in the church and yet far from the kingdom. I was preaching in a revival in a southern city at the peak of the civil rights controversy. During the song service a Negro entered the sanctuary and was ushered down to a front seat. Two choir members immediately walked out in protest. In so doing they not only left the worshiping community of God, but they moved far away from the kingdom of God! For if prejudice and hatred so filled their hearts that they could not sit in the same church service with a black brother in Christ, how could they expect to abide forever in the eternal kingdom of God in fellowship with these and other believers of all races!

The *self-righteous* man is far from the kingdom. Jesus told of two men who went into the Temple to pray (Luke 18:10). The Pharisee stood with head lifted up and arms outstretched crying, "I thank God I am not as other men. I pray. I tithe. I practice my religion daily!" I hear this prayer frequently, both inside the church and out. "Thank God, I am not a hypocrite like that rascal of a deacon that I know." "At least, I am better than most people who join the church and profess religion."

So Jesus said the self-righteous Pharisee prayed "unto himself," thanking God that he was at least better than others—and much better than the sinful publican standing to the side. But the publican prayed with bowed head and penitent heart, "Lord, be merciful unto me a sinner." When the prayer meeting was over, Jesus said the penitent humble publican had entered into the kingdom of God but the self-righteous Pharisee was still afar off.

The *self-sufficient* person is far from the kingdom. I talked to an affluent successful young man who said, "I need nothing! I am doing all right for myself in life. Religion doesn't hold a thing for me!" I thought, any faith, or no faith at all, will do when skies are fair, when the sea is calm, when life moves on under the sail of health and youth and hope and promise. But what happens when the storm breaks and the stygian darkness of hopelessness and despair settles on your soul? What about that day when life goes to pieces? The baby dies? Your health and youth are threatened by an incurable disease? The security of your marriage shattered by infidelity? Your job lost? Your home gone?

Life is not all sunshine! There are tears and shadows and sorrows. And you will come to a day when you suddenly discover that you cannot conquer life by yourself! There are circumstances and situations beyond your control. And in that day, your faith in a personal and loving God is your only source of strength and hope! But the self-sufficient person who feels *no need* for God is far from the kingdom.

The *materialist* is far from the kingdom—that person who pitches his life at the animal level and lives for the present world. Gallio, the Roman procurator for the city of Corinth, heard the great apostle Paul but "Gallio cared for none of those things" (Acts 18:17). So there are many like Gallio that do not care for the church, for the Word of God, for religious and spiritual things. And like Gallio, they are far from the kingdom.

The person who has committed the *unpardonable* sin is far from the kingdom! That person who has deliberately and willfully resisted the call of God again and again, and has denied the Spirit of God again and again—that person has moved farther from the kingdom with every rejection.

Jesus was surrounded by some Pharisees that Jesus said were so far from the kingdom that they were without hope! The Bible says, *"They could not believe!"* (John 12:39). The Pharisees were so solidified and hardened in their self-righteousness, self-adequacy, and bitterness . . . and had resisted the invitation of Christ to believe so many times—that they had lost the sensitivity, the capacity to respond to the call of the kingdom! I believe this is what is meant by the unpardonable sin: willful resistance to the Spirit of God, so often repeated that the sinner's heart is hardened and he loses the *capacity* to respond to God's love! I believe the unpardonable sin is not an *act;* it is a *condition* brought about by many deliberate acts. It is a hardening, until all sensitivity to God is gone. It is not that God *will not pardon and forgive*, but the man *cannot repent*; and without repentance there can be no forgiveness. The *hardened heart* is far from the kingdom.

Some Are *Not* Far

But how Jesus' heart must have leapt within him as he saw this lawyer. "But thou art *not far* from the kingdom!" What was the difference between this lawyer and the Pharisee? What is the difference today between those who are far off and you who are not far from the kingdom?

First, Jesus sensed in this man a feeling of *need.* He was open, looking, and searching for something. He wanted a supreme law, a fixed star outside himself and beyond himself to guide his life by! He wanted a standard set by God himself by which he could measure his life.

This is the beginning point of faith: *a sense of need.* Only when the sick man acknowledges his need for treatment, only then can a doctor help him. Only when a sinner acknowledges a need for a spiritual experience, only then can God help him. God cannot enter the closed heart. God cannot speak to the muffled ear. God cannot change the mind that has already fixed its choice. God cannot come into the self-satisfied life.

But God can deal with a person who is open, who is seeking, who is questing, who is yearning, even as you are.

Second, the lawyer recognized the *futility* and emptiness of the forms of organized religion that he witnessed in the Temple area.

A long-haired young person found a seat near the front in a very formal church service. As a scholarly minister slowly and deliberately read his sermon from a manuscript, the young person began to punctuate his statements about Jesus Christ with a hearty "Amen," much to the distraction of the minister. Presently an usher quietly slipped down the aisle, tapped the young man on the shoulder and said, "You must be quiet—you are disturbing the pastor." The young man whispered, "But he's talking about Jesus, and I just had to say amen. I've got religion!" The usher sternly replied, "Well, you didn't get it *here,* so sit down and be quiet!" So, sometimes our formal expressions of religion are quite empty of real meaning.

I am not condemning the orderly and organized expression of religion. As the physical body has many parts organized into multiple functions, so the body of Christ must have structure and form and organization to be effective. But there is always the tendency for form and structure to stifle the spirit.

It is easy for ceremonialism to become one's religion. It is symbolic. Unintentionally, a symbol frequently used, may in time seem to be the real thing. The danger is just that—that the thing signified is lost sight of in the symbol itself. We have much of this in Christianity today. *Rites* and *rituals* have become "saving acts." *Symbolic physical things* have acquired *saving efficacy*—water, bread, sacred relics, images, a church structure!

So the lawyer was saying, "Right you are, Lord. True religion is certainly not in ritual and sacrifice, in holy days and feast days! It is not how you stand and sing. Or when you kneel and pray! It is not the way you observe the ordinances! It is not even how you have been baptized! It is not even *who* baptized you! It is not a piece of bread that opens the door to the kingdom. It is not a drop of water that imparts citizenship in the kingdom. The door to the church, by whatever name, is not the door to the kingdom. True religion is the measure of love in your heart for God and the expression of that love toward your fellowman!

"Love the Lord thy God with *all thy heart!*" When Sir Walter Raleigh was led to the block, his executioners asked him if his head lay right. Raleigh answered, "It matters little, my friend, how the head lies, provided the heart is right." That is what counts!

Being Near Is Not in the Kingdom

Jesus said, "Thou art not far from the kingdom." The lawyer was living in the suburbs. What else was needful to enter the kingdom? Already he had given intellectual agreement to Jesus definition of true religion. But to affirm your religious faith *intellectually* is not enough! Already he had *emotionally* responded by turning away in disgust from legalism and coming with an open heart to Jesus. But to emotionally respond to religion is not enough! There is yet one more step to cross over the line and into the kingdom!

Imagine that inside each of us are three little men. They sit at a judgment bar determining the direction of life. The first little man is *intellect.* He controls the mind. He says, "I believe that Jesus Christ is the Son of God . . . born at Bethlehem . . . died on the cross . . . was resurrected. I believe he is the Savior, the Bible is the Word of God, and men must come to him to be saved." But this little man, intellect, alone does not control us. To only intellectually accept the facts about Jesus Christ is not adequate for saving faith.

The second little man is *emotion.* He controls our feelings. He says, "I feel so lost . . . so wicked . . . so unhappy. . . . I feel that Jesus loves me and I want to love him." But an emotional response to the love of God and the cross of Christ is not enough.

The third little man is *will!* And both emotion and intellect must wait for the vote of this third little man. He says, "I will. I commit. I act. I surrender!"

You may believe with your mind and feel with your heart, but you do not become a Christian until you have also committed yourself to Jesus Christ. At a *definite time,* at a *definite place* you must *definitely say,* "I *believe* in Jesus Christ, I *love* him. *And I commit myself to him!*"

On a certain day at a certain time my daughter and a young man stood before me. They had consented in their *minds* that they belonged to each other. Their *hearts* had given confirmation of emotion and love to this union. Yet they stood at the altar still unmarried—waiting to take the final step. At a definite time, in a definite place, they made a definite commitment of life to each other. "I give myself . . . I take you." It was the *commitment of will,* made in the presence of God and sealed by the Holy Spirit, that united two lives into one in holy matrimony and established for them a new relationship.

In like manner, you must come into the presence of God at a definite time and place with a definite commitment of will, "I love Jesus. I believe in him. And here, now, I take Jesus Christ as my Savior and I give myself to him." At the same moment Jesus Christ comes to stand at your side to say, "I accept you as the one I died for on the cross, and give myself to you." At that moment the Jesus Christ whom you have accepted intellectually as a historical figure of 2,000 years ago, suddenly becomes a living resurrected presence, eternally linked to you in a new relationship and an everlasting union.

For you to be so near to the kingdom and not come in *today,* could mean that you would be eternally lost.

The *Royal Charter* was the queen of the seas of her day. She sailed in glory around the world with the elite of Europe on board. Returning from her triumphant voyage, she was sighted at eventide just off Queenstown. The message was quickly passed overland to the home port of Liverpool, "The *Royal Charter* will dock in the morning." The mayor came to greet her. Bands gathered to play. Crowds lined the wharf to meet the passengers and crew. But sometime during the night, between Queenstown and Liverpool, the *Royal Charter* ran aground and went down. Hundreds were drowned!

Dr. William Taylor, a renowned pastor of that day, went to the home to tell the wife of the first mate that he had been lost at sea. She greeted the pastor, "Come in. You can have breakfast with us as we welcome my husband home. He is on the *Royal Charter* and it docks this morning!" When Dr. Taylor broke the tragic news that her husband was drowned she cried, "Oh, God, he was *so near* . . . and lost! So near and lost!" What a tragedy it would be for you to be so near to the kingdom of God today and not enter in—and go into eternity *lost!*

You are *so near* to the kingdom. Take the final step today and enter in!

John Wesley, the father of Methodism, made history wholesale! Historians say that the religious revolution begun in England by the Wesleys is of greater historic importance than the military victories of England during the same period. Yet this devout and intensely pious man lived the earlier part of his life near to but outside the kingdom of God . . . even while he tried to be a minister and missionary.

His daily Journal of May 24, 1738, records what happened. He returned from America as a missionary to the Indians only to discover "what I least of all expected, that I who went to America to convert the Indians, was never myself converted to God!" Groping and searching for a vital personal experience with the living God and peace of heart to know that his sins were forgiven, Wesley wrote, "I resolve to seek it unto the end." On that Wednesday of May 24, he found it! In the morning, he had opened his Bible haphazardly and it fell open to this verse, "Thou art not far from the kingdom of God!"

He was reassured—the kingdom of God—not far! But how far? He continues to write, "In the evening I went very unwillingly to a society on Aldersgate Street, where one was reading Luther's preface of the epistle to the Romans. About a quarter before nine, while he was describing the change which works in the heart through faith in Christ, *I felt my heart strangely warmed.*

I felt I did trust in Christ, Christ alone, for salvation; and assurance was given me that he had taken away my sins, even mine, and saved me from the laws of sin and death."

And on that same evening, John Wesley passed out of the suburbs through the gates of life into the kingdom of God. Even as you too may enter into life in his kingdom today by the personal commitment of your life to Jesus Christ.

XII

How to Begin Again

Jeremiah 18:1-6

Louisa Tarkington wistfully wrote:

"I wish that there were some wonderful place
Called the Land of Beginning Again:
Where all our mistakes and all our heartaches
And all of our poor selfish grief
Could be dropped like a shabby old coat at the door
And never put on again. . . ."

That is precisely what a young man was saying as he spoke of bright dreams, a grand start and the promise of a brilliant career. But his voice quivered in bitter confession, "I have messed up my life; how I wish I could start over again!"

That is what a brokenhearted woman was saying as she said that her husband of twenty years had left her for a younger woman. "How can I pick up the broken pieces and start over again?"

That is the quest of a weary world seeking a way out of depravity, war, hatred, and injustice and looking for a new beginning of brotherhood and justice.

That was the question of the weeping prophet, Jeremiah, 2,700 years ago. He saw his beloved nation revelling in sin and pursuing pleasure. The prophet wondered, "Have we drifted beyond the forgiveness and redemption of God?" Is there any hope for a new beginning?"

In the Potter's House

God says to Jeremiah, "Go to Jericho for an answer to your question." I see the prophet as he hurries from Jerusalem. His flowing robe billows behind him in his haste to find this sage of wisdom, this scholar of Scriptures who will speak for God. Imagine the prophet's surprise when he discovers that God's spokesman is an humble potter. And God will speak through the man's *actions* and not his words.

Jeremiah stands in the shadows of the workshop and watches the silent master at work. Three objects catch his eye.

First, there is the *potter* himself. He scoops from the pit a handful of clay and shapes it into a ball. The prophet sees the application. That is God forming man of the dust of the earth. Every human life is the result of the purposeful creative hand of God that has scooped us out of the clay pit and given us personhood, identity, and individuality. He also sees the potter as God choosing Israel out of the mass of humanity to make of her a nation.

Then Jeremiah's eyes focus on the potter's *wheel.* That is the spinning wheel of time and circumstance. Some would say that this spinning wheel is the only determining factor in life—the wheel of *fortune.* So they explain life in terms of *fate* and blind *chance* saying, "That's the way the ball bounces—the way the cookie crumbles." But Jeremiah observes that the potter does not abandon the clay after it is thrown onto the spinning wheel. When God chose Israel, he did not abandon her. Neither has God abandoned your life nor my life to the spinning circumstances of fate. He sees the potter with nimble fingers begin to shape the clay as it spins on the wheel.

The prophet's attention then focuses on the *clay.* It is inert, a shapeless mass. It is helpless without the touch of the potter's hand to achieve anything of beauty or worth in and of itself. Even as there can be no real worth achieved, no full development of our capacities, no fashioning of eternal beauty in our lives, of ourselves and by ourselves apart from the touch of God!

So our beginnings are more than an evolutionary march out of a pit of clay; life is more than the wheel of blind chance and impersonal fate spinning us; and our true destiny is to be achieved only by the divine touch of the Master's hand.

The Master at Work

So Jeremiah stands intrigued by this potter who has captured the attention of clear-eyed men of all generations. Isaiah, Zechariah, and the apostle Paul learned of him. Omar Khayam, the eleventh-century Persian bard, and Robert Browning, the English poet wrote of him.

The potter is a *busy worker.* His flying feet propel the spinning wheel faster, his nimble fingers knead and shape the clay. Our sovereign God is no absentee landowner, lounging in a far-off mansion, indifferent to the affairs of his earthly plantation. Our creative God did not make this world and then abandon it to operate by a mathematical formula. He is imminent and present in every fiber of his creation. His finger is in every event of life and every circumstance of history. A man said as he opened his newspaper, "Let's see what God has been doing in his world today."

That is the bold affirmation of the Bible—philosophy of history declaring that God has been at work in his world since its beginnings. The Bible is an account of God's mighty redemptive acts and demonstrations of power as he has dealt with men at various times and in various places. And it tells of his ultimate intervention in history in Jesus Christ! How we need to be aware of this today! God rules! God reigns! And God is still at *work* in his world regardless of how confused the circumstances might seem.

The potter is working *individually,* with one piece of clay. So our God is more than a great cosmic mind, the first cause, some mystical life force; he is a *personal* God who deals with us personally as *individuals* on a one-to-one basis!

He is the God of detail who cares about the smallest aspects of the most insignificant life. We have a martin house in our backyard—which unfortunately the martins have ignored! But I have had great success attracting a huge flock of pesky sparrows!

Recently I found on the ground a tiny baby sparrow that had fallen from the birdhouse. It was dead, an ugly thing; with it's big head, and tiny naked body and its two feet sticking straight up. I gingerly picked it up to toss it into the garbage can when I remembered what Jesus had said that *not even a sparrow falls to earth but that my heavenly Father knows* (Matt. 10:29). Suddenly, that grotesque little thing became a sacred symbol of God's personal care and concern about me—and you—and every little trivial thing in our lives!

The potter is working *constructively*. He is making something beautiful and worthwhile. So our God is always at the business of touching us to make us better, to make our lives more beautiful. Yet how often we think of our Christian faith only in terms of negatives: what we must give up, or what is denied us of the pleasures of life. Or how often we try to measure righteousness and godliness in negative terms of sins not committed.

When I was a pastor in the Appalachian Mountains, many of our churches practiced "church discipline." Members guilty of misconduct such as immorality, drunkenness, and sometimes dancing and playing cards, were called before the congregation and turned out! And as a young preacher I am afraid I often thought that my best sermons were those that *skinned* everybody, saved and sinner alike. But the years have taught me that the chastisement of church discipline seldom redeems a faltering church member! And for every sinner who needs skinning, there are scores who need the assurance of God's love, the promise of God's forgiveness, the warmth of our acceptance, and the hope that by the power of God they can make a new start in life.

The Bible says that "God sent not his Son into the world to *condemn* the world; but that the world through him might be *saved!*" God's purpose is not to destroy men. He is ever at work trying to save, to restore, to build up, and make new men for this world of his.

This is what God wants to do for you personally, today. And

as God touches you, it will be as with the potter, to shape you, and make of you something more wonderful. Let him touch your life and he will make a better person of you! Let him touch your marriage and home and it will be a happier relationship. Let him touch your work and he will enrich it and bring glory and happiness into the daily grind of things. Remember, it is never a mistake to take a step toward God, toward his church—in surrender, in renewal, in rededication! It is never a mistake to yield to the touch of God! He always touches us for the better!

The potter is working *intelligently*, shaping the clay into a pattern, preconceived in his mind. Behind every life, yours and mine, is a Master architect with a plan and a design! God himself has a blueprint and a will for every life. And the highest achievement of life is for you to find and do the will of God in your life!

The Broken Vessel

Jeremiah stands fascinated by the potter, the wheel, and the beautiful vessel being shaped from the clay. Suddenly, the vessel flies to pieces. The potter's workmanship is destroyed! Jeremiah wonders, "Why this failure?" Not the potter, he is still the master craftsman! Not the wheel, it still spins. Something in the clay resisted, a chip of gravel, an unyielding grain of sand. And because something in the clay resisted the master's touch, he failed!

Herein is an awesome truth! You and I, finite beings, can thwart the purpose of the Almighty God! We can resist and rebel and cause God himself to fail in our lives!

So Adam and Eve in the Garden of Eden resisted the authority of God in their lives when they disobeyed God's commandment. And from Adam to this day, the workmanship of God in our lives is marred because of this same sin of rebellion and self-will and resistance to the authority of God over our lives!

Jeremiah turns to go. He has the message from God! Declare to Israel, "God wanted to do something with you, but you resisted.

Now the vessel is broken, God's purpose thwarted! You have lost your destiny!"

A Second Touch

But God calls Jeremiah back. The lesson is not finished. The potter is not through with the marred vessel. He watches the master gather every fragment of the broken vessel and knead the clay again into a ball. Once more he throws it onto the potter's wheel. With deft fingers he quickly shapes it, and brings forth a vessel more beautiful than the first. As the potter lifts the vessel, redeemed by his second effort, for the approval of Jeremiah, the prophet hears the voice of God asking, "O Israel, cannot I do with you even as this potter?"

This is the glorious promise of the gospel. How many times we have resisted the will of God! How many shattered vessels and dismal failures there have been! But God is not through! Your life is still in his hands. He wants to give you a new beginning and make for you a new life.

These are three steps for you to take in faith to experience a second touch from the hand of God today!

First, believe in the purpose of God at work in this world, and in your life.

It is a cold dark night on the Pennsylvania Canal. A teenage deckhand on the towboat *The Evening Star* takes his turn at the bowline. As he uncoils the rope, it catches in a crevice on the edge of the deck. The sleepy boy gives a tug to free it. As he throws his weight against the line, it slips loose and throws him backward into the dark waters of the canal. He frantically clutches the loose rope that has fallen into the water with him. Again, the rope catches a second time in a crevice on the deck and the boy slowly pulls himself back on board.

Sitting there in the darkness, he contemplates his narrow escape and the miracle that saved him. He tries to fling the rope into the crevice where it had twice caught, once to throw him into the dark waters, and a second time to pull him out of his watery grave. He tries to fling the rope into the crevice. Six hundred times, again and again, he tries. But it never will catch. He is convinced that only the miraculous hand of God saved him from a watery grave.

Believing that God has some purpose for his life, he resolves to go home, get an education and be something more than a riverboat laborer. He makes his way overland across Ohio and comes in the evening to his mother's cabin in the woods. Looking in the window, he sees her beside the fireplace, reading the Bible. And he hears her praying aloud and quoting Psalm 86:16: "O turn unto me, and have mercy upon me; give thy strength unto thy servant, and save the son of thine handmaid." The boy rushes in and falls at her feet, telling how God has miraculously saved him and how he had committed himself to the will of God.

He goes on to receive his education, become president of a college, to serve with distinction in the Civil War, is elected to Office and enters the White House as James A. Garfield, President of the United States!

Yes, God had a purpose for a towboat deckhand. Even as God had a purpose for a plowboy named Elisha on whose shoulders the mantle of the great prophet Elijah would fall. God had a purpose for the misguided zealot Saul holding the coats of the mob that stoned Stephen. God had a purpose for a babe named Moses hidden in the bulrushes of the Nile River. God had a purpose for a disobedient and runaway preacher named Jonah. God had a purpose for a sixteen-year-old girl who sang in the choir of a country church who became a missionary in spite of the opposition of parents. God had a purpose for a ten-year-old boy passing out revival handbills in the bars of a mountain town and declaring that God had called him to the ministry. And God has a purpose for your life, too. God has something good and wonderful that he wants to do for you and through you. Believe *that* today, and never rest until you have found that purpose and are fully surrendered to do his will in your life.

Second, believe in the patience of God. You are discouraged! You have failed God so many times! You have started over again and again! And you ask, "Will God really give me another chance?"

Robert Ingersoll, the eloquent atheist of another generation, often stood before an audience declaring, "I will prove there is no God." Then, holding up his watch, he would challenge God to strike him dead in the next 60 seconds! As the seconds ticked by, he taunted God and profaned God. Men screamed and women fainted as the tension built and they waited for Almighty God to strike down the blasphemer. When the time was gone, Colonel Ingersoll would drop the watch into his pocket and laugh, "You see, there is no God!" When Joseph Parker, the English minister, visited America and saw Colonel Ingersoll so challenge God, he merely commented, "Who does this puny American think he is—that he can exhaust the eternal patience of a loving God in 60 seconds!"

There is *not one person* listening today, regardless of what you have done, who has exhausted the love and patience of God. You simply cannot go beyond the love of God. God loves you and keeps on loving you. He forgives you and will keep on forgiving you, whenever you will respond to him in true repentance.

Finally, accept the promise of God. Hear the wonderful words declared to Jeremiah, "Can not I do with you as this potter? Behold, as clay in the potter's hand, so are you in my hands."

Joseph Medill, in his reminiscences of the great Lincoln-Douglas debate, recalls a friend pleading with Douglas not to make the speech which later would be his political ruin. Douglas would not be persuaded. He made his choice and set his course. But after Civil War swept the land, Douglas saw his great mistake, and was overwhelmed by remorse and grief. Dying of fever his biographer, Medill, says he heard Douglas whispering, "I missed it! I missed it! I missed it!"

It is not God's will that any one should miss the way to eternal and abundant life today. He stands before you not only as the God of the second chance, but the seventh chance and the seventieth chance! With unlimited love and patience he is ready to forgive and redeem and reshape and make all things new in your life. But he is subject to your will, your response, your decision! By yielding to him in confession, repentance and faith, he will make you over and you can begin again, today!